# KEEP YOUR COOL WHEN PARENTING TEENS

## 7 HACKS TO SET HEALTHY BOUNDARIES, LECTURE LESS, LISTEN MORE, AND BUILD A STRONG RELATIONSHIP

### DAVID SKIDDY

# CONTENTS

# A GIFT TO OUR READERS

Included with your purchase of this book is our short Parents'
Guide
**How To Help Your Teen Fight Anxiety, Stress and
Depression**

**Scan QR code or visit:**

**keepyourcool.littlegeckopublishing.com**

# INTRODUCTION

"The first few weeks are the worst."

"The 'terrible twos' are a nightmare."

"Just wait until they get a bit older."

It seems that every stage of childhood comes with a new daunting warning from parents who have come before us. They may think they are helping, but most times, it only serves to fill us with more anxiety about something we already find intimidating.

Surprisingly, the teenage years come with little warning and are often the time when parents find themselves completely stumped. This stage comes with a unique set of characteristics that make it nearly impossible to continue effectively parenting your child. And doing so without completely shattering your relationship with them is simply out of the question, right?

Where exactly does the line between child and adult lie with teenagers? How much privacy and responsibility is too much, and how much is not enough? How do I treat them as an adult when they still misbehave and make childish mistakes? How do I talk to them when all they do is ignore me?

Trying to parent a teenager can feel like living with the most irresponsible and infuriating roommate. What happened to the little angel who would listen when you told them to be careful? What happened to the baby who would squeal with joy when you hugged them? When did that child become the teenager who ignores your advice and shrugs away from your touch? When did this happen?

It is one of the most challenging things to watch your child grow up, develop their sense of identity and independence, and no longer rely on you as much as they used to. Suddenly, the toddler who needed help tying their shoelaces is a teenager who doesn't even want your help with their homework.

It is easy to feel like you're doing everything wrong, especially when your teenager doesn't have a problem telling you as much. You're doing your absolute best to be there for them and ensure they have a happy and healthy adolescence because your teenage years left something to be desired. But they are not interested in your assistance and are seemingly unafraid to tell you.

Your teenager is growing up, and you're watching them make mistakes; either the same mistakes you made at their age or completely new mistakes of their own. You can tell when your teenager is having a bad day or something deeply upsets them.

You can tell when your teenager is no longer happy; all they can feel is anger or something worse. And they simply won't let you help. Your hands are tied.

You are not alone. I feel confident in saying that *every* parent struggles with the teenage years. Each teenager is unique and uniquely tricky to deal with. You may have a teenager who is a wound-up ball of anger, one comment away fro

m unraveling completely. You may have a teenager who is becoming involved in risky activities that you would much rather they avoid. You may have a teenager struggling to find their place in this world, which is starting to affect their mental well-being. You may have a teenager so concerned with achieving success that they have forgotten how to enjoy life, trapped under the heavy weight of anxiety.

Teenagers face an incredible number of obstacles in life once adolescence and puberty hit. They are so overwhelmed and over-stimulated by their ever-changing life that being a well-behaved child who appreciates and listens to their parents becomes a non-priority. Without the guidance of a parent, these tough years can have a serious impact on their mental well-being, their confidence, and their future. But they don't know that. They are convinced they can do it on their own.

Don't let them.

Do not let your teenager do this on their own. As a parent, you have to be there for them. As a parent, you must be strong and hold your ground, even when they push you away as hard as possible. They do need you, and they do love you. As much as it feels like you have lost your little angel, they are still there and are now learning to fly with their newfound wings. If you let them do it on their own, they will fall. They need your help and your guidance.

In this book, I hope to offer the tools you need to be there for your teenager. I hope to impart to you the knowledge required to handle every obstacle with clarity. And I hope to help you get through the teenage years without losing the special bond between parent and child.

# 1

# PARENTING TEENS 101

Jill Churchill (1992) said, "There is no way to be a perfect mother and a million ways to be a good one." There is no fool-proof way to parent any child, let alone a teenager. Everyone has their own method. Even if you are using a tried and tested technique, you will need to adjust certain things to your circumstance and teenager. There are many ways to parent a teenager, but there are a few standard building blocks on which every technique is based.

## LEARN HOW ...

### ... Independent Your Teen Should Be

Learning to give your teenager the room to be independent and make their own decisions can be very difficult, especially when you have to watch your child walk head-first into a huge mistake. It can be a balancing act to determine just how much autonomy to allow your teen.

Teenagers still rely on their parents regarding morality, beliefs, and values—doing the "right thing." They should still be held accountable for doing the "wrong thing," such as lying, stealing, or mistreating someone. However, they do need more independence in expressing themselves, such as their clothes or which friends or activities they choose to spend their time on.

Learning to "let go" of your unimportant differences of opinions—such as what your teen is wearing or who they are hanging out with—will help to avoid unnecessary arguments. It will also allow for more critical conversations, such as respect and responsibilities.

It may be difficult to step back and let your child make their own decisions, but—as a parent—you need to be ready at a moment's notice to help them deal with consequences for which they are unprepared.

### ... To Help Your Teen Make Good Decisions

Research (AACAP, 2016) shows that teenagers' brains physically work differently than the brains of adults. Teenagers are much more likely to act impulsively, failing to think before they act. They are more likely to misunderstand social cues or even their own emotions. This means that a teenager's idea of a "good decision" is wildly different from an adult's.

It's unfair to expect your teenager to problem-solve the same way you would or to thoroughly think through every decision they make. They are not built to function in that way. It is unlikely that teens will take a moment to evaluate the possible consequences of their actions, and they are even less likely to change their behavior accordingly.

Now is the best time to start teaching and enforcing critical thinking skills to help them make good decisions. Start helping your teenager analyze their situation and see the possible consequences of behaving in one way or another. Learning to make good decisions comes from understanding what a bad decision is. And that only happens after you have made a couple of bad choices for yourself and personally experience the consequences thereof.

So, do not expect your teenager to make sound decisions right from the beginning. Making mistakes is part of the teenage experience. Give your teenager the space to make theirs. Always be ready and available to help them correct their errors or to help them deal with the consequences of their actions. But guarding your teenager against making any mistakes *ever* only serves to shield them from reality. This, in turn, will actually stunt your teenager's ability to learn from their mistakes.

If your teenager is heading toward a wrong decision, begin a conversation about the consequences and reasons for making such a decision rather than aggressively steering them away from it. Your teenager will not do this independently, so make a space for them to do so.

### *... To Convince Your Teen to Listen*

The first step to ensuring your teenager listens when you speak is simply to listen when they do. How often are you so concerned with ensuring your teenager obeys you that you don't focus on what they are trying to say? When your child was younger, you could listen to their stories for hours; be willing to do the same with your teenager.

I can understand the urge to advise and correct their behavior because, as adults, we think we know better. And we probably do. However, instead of convincing them that we are right, take the time to listen to their argument and struggles. The most important thing to remember is this: Do not judge. Just listen. If you want your teenager to show you respect, you must do the same.

Another reason teenagers might be unlikely to listen to you is that you might not practice what you preach. Parents are sometimes so focused on their teenagers' behavior that they don't stop to think about their own. How often do you tell your teenager not to procrastinate, but your own to-do list is a mile long? How often do you tell your teen to prioritize their friendships, yet you haven't seen your friends in months? How many times have you said drinking affects your health while sitting with a glass of wine in your hand?

Teenagers won't listen to someone they are afraid of becoming. Your teenager is watching you: how you behave, how you feel about life, and how you treat those around you. You need to be a role model, an example to your teenager. If you are bored with life, avoid your friends, and leave important tasks undone for weeks, why would your teenager listen to you and risk becoming the same way?

Furthermore, analyze how you react when your teenager does something wrong. Would you want to listen to someone who only freaks out when you've made a mistake? Getting your teenager to listen actually involves a lot of keeping your mouth shut. Do not try to fix or reprimand at every turn. Learn to react with clarity and calmness, and your teenager will be much more likely to listen when you speak.

### ... To Get Through the Years Without Your Teen Hating You

This phase of "hating" you happens when a teenager is trying to find independence. Often, teenagers are not even sure how exactly to find it. The first step *must* be detaching from those on whom they depend—their parents. That's why teenagers distance themselves and create that barrier because they feel it holds them back from finding independence.

To help counteract this detachment and hatred, you need to support and encourage their freedom. This could be allowing your teenager more responsibilities, involving them in challenging household chores/tasks, or allowing them to make more decisions on their own, which enables them to test and show their capabilities.

When a teenager expresses anger and hatred toward you, it may be their way of testing the waters—seeing just how much they can get away with and how much you will allow. The key is to continue being firm but loving. Often, a teenager's words can hurt so badly that we want to react with rejection or similar detachment. But this shows your teenager that you wouldn't love them at their worst. You need to stand your ground—not allowing disrespect, but you also need to show them that you will love and support them through everything, even hurtful words.

Another great way to help your teenager find their independence in a healthy way is to allow them to have their own experiences outside of the family and the house. Allow your teenager to go on camping trips, internships, etc., and allow them to live and exist in the world without you. This will expose them to life without their parent. Of course, this should only be done safely, where your child's well-being is not threatened or at risk.

## THE AWKWARD IN-BETWEEN

Adolescence is a phase when someone is no longer a child but not yet an adult. These years can be confusing for your teenager and everyone around them. How should they be treated and dealt with? How much independence or responsibility should they have? They're old enough for certain things but much too young for others.

Do you remember another time when your child was in a transitional stage of life, moody and difficult to deal with, and when your sweet angel was no longer a baby but not quite a child yet? The infamous toddler years.

The more you think about it, the more pronounced the similarities between toddlers and teenagers become.

### *Basic Needs*

Just like toddlers, teenagers have basic physical needs that should be met. We're talking about getting fed, keeping clean, staying active, getting to bed on time, etc. However, toddlers need help with every step of this process. They don't know what they need and rely on us to provide it.

Teenagers are much more aware of what they need. After learning to take care of themselves, they now know how to do it. You would think this means less involvement is required from the parents, but you would be incorrect. Teenagers may understand what they should do, but personal care may not be their highest priority. Teenagers are so preoccupied with the other facets of their life—like their social life or school—that taking care of themselves becomes an afterthought.

At the very least, we still must provide our teenagers with food, but it will probably take more than that. Teenagers must be reminded (but not nagged) about taking showers, going to bed on time, or staying active. It's important to remember that, because of their need for independence, teenagers don't want to be told what to do. This is especially true when it's something as "childish" as going to bed or eating all their food. A reminder might need to come in the form of a question such as, "I'm starving. Are you ready for dinner?" or "I'm exhausted. What time were you going to head to bed?"

*Structure*

Another need that is similar between toddlers and teenagers is structure. Just as toddlers need a schedule to help them feel secure and learn consistency, the same is true with teenagers. Unfortunately, teenagers' lives are jam-packed with many more activities than toddlers'. School, homework, studying, extra-curricular activities, friends, dates, driving, parties, and the like can be overwhelming for a teenager. They need help learning how and what to prioritize.

The key difference between a toddler and a teenager in terms of structure, however, is that a toddler has everything planned out for them while a teenager is expected to manage on their own. A toddler is airlifted from their very successful animal farm to a personal stylist, put into a metal can that moves a million miles an hour, and then dropped off at some colorful building with a bunch of other toddlers and a teacher who is always smiling. Later, Mom or Dad picks them up, feeds them lunch, plays for a while, bathes them, and then puts them in bed. They have no idea what the next hour of their life holds, nor do they care. Toddlers are somewhat forced to go with the flow.

On the other hand, teenagers are hyperaware of just how little time there is in a day. They must go to school, study and do homework, wash their hair, watch 17 hours of Netflix, and somehow find time to go on that date. And it's worse on the weekend when friends want to see friends, but no one has a method of transportation. That's when we get asked—on the morning of—if we can drive to twelve different suburbs and three different malls.

This can be infuriating with a teenager who doesn't care about your plans for the weekend, is horrendous at communicating effectively, and is ungrateful (and usually irritated) that you gave up your time to drive them around.

It can also lead to hours of time set aside for studying but none for self-care, or they could devote hours to socializing but none to homework.

The problem is that teenagers are expected to plan out their whole lives when they have never been taught how to. We expect teenagers to tell us when parties are being held, where the parties are, and who the party is for, but we never tell them what information we want or how far in advance we want it. We expect teenagers to plan a healthy, balanced lifestyle when they don't even know what that looks like.

If you have never included them in household chores—cooking, cleaning, or doing laundry—you must be patient and proactive. You cannot expect that, after blowing out the candles on their 13th birthday, they will suddenly offer to make supper for the house, do their laundry, walk the dog, and pack their lunch for school. You can't expect these things to fall into place just because your child has gotten older.

Have you taught your teenager how to manage their time? Do they know when to communicate with you about their plans? Have they seen what a healthy balance in their life should look like?

If you would like to, I have a book dedicated to teaching teenagers about critical thinking, time management, and goal setting. This might be a valuable resource to help your children learn to organize their time effectively.

### Safety

It doesn't matter if your child is three or thirty; you will always be concerned about their safety and well-being. However, once again, there is a stark difference in how we deal with a toddler and a teenager.

With toddlers, we play an active role in protecting them and preventing any situation threatening their safety and well-being. With teenagers, we let them out into the world and can only hope they make the right decisions. We hope they don't put themselves in danger or threaten their own well-being, but like toddlers, teenagers are prone to making unnecessarily risky decisions. With teenagers, we simply hope we have taught them well.

Teenagers are exposed to many more risky situations than a toddler: i.e. peer pressure in terms of drugs and alcohol, bullying, unsafe sex, car accidents (if your teenager is driving), stress and anxiety, and much more.

### Other Similarities

- Toddlers and teenagers both go through a considerable spike in **cognitive function and development**. Toddlers are learning to interact with the world, talk, walk, etc. Teenagers are learning to be a part of the world, communicate, be productive, comprehend and control their emotions, take care of themselves, etc.

- Because their world is moving so fast around them, and everything is rapidly changing, both teenagers and toddlers tend to be hugely **self-centered**. Their world is so demanding of their attention that anything that doesn't have to do with them is unimportant.

- Teenagers and toddlers are both very **social** beings. They have friends, they want friends, and they spend time with friends. Toddlers are learning to be a friend and part of a team, whereas teenagers must learn to be an individual despite the influence of their friends.

- Both toddlers and teenagers are eager to be **independent** and do things on their own without the help of their parents. For toddlers, it can be playing by themselves, eating by themselves, or even getting dressed without help. For teenagers, it's simply existing without their parents or finding out who they are as individuals.

- It's no surprise that toddlers and teenagers are both wildly **adventurous and risk-taking**. Toddlers will happily jump off a swing to see how far they can fly, and teenagers will consider trying out a drug "just to see how it feels." However, the reasoning is quite different. Toddlers simply don't know any better. Teenagers are trying to find their personality and identity, and they'll try anything once to see how it fits in with who they are or want to be.

## PARENTING STYLES

It's important to note that parenting skills can be learned. They are not innately within every one of us, and it's never too late to learn these new skills and put them into practice. As parents, we must understand that we cannot *fix* our teenagers because there is nothing to *fix*. However, what we can do is change our behavior because our reactions and our words will directly affect our children's behavior. We can work on building a more positive atmosphere and ensure that essential communication lines remain open.

There are four defined parenting styles with their own advantages and disadvantages, which we will examine in the following sections. While reading, analyze your current parenting challenge and imagine how certain parenting styles may help you achieve your goal.

### Authoritarian

Authoritarian parenting is a style of parenting that focuses on rules, structure, and discipline. These parents are very strict and place extreme expectations on their children. When their child misbehaves or makes a mistake, they default to shaming them, yelling at them, or even resorting to corporal punishment.

Nurturing their children is not a priority for authoritarian parents. If it happens, it is only when their children are well-behaved. And "well-behaved" is a lofty goal because these parents are very impatient regarding misbehavior.

The negatives that come from authoritarian parenting outweigh the positives. Such strict parenting and high expectations serve to put children under an extreme amount of stress and anxiety. Children with such discipline often seek ways to rebel and test their limits. Some studies (Dewar, 2017) show other adverse side effects of raising children with an authoritarian parenting style, such as a tendency to bully peers, lack of empathy, and lower social competence.

The authoritarian parenting method does not allow children to have freedom or practice responsibility. It doesn't let teenagers think for themselves because parents constantly tell them what, how, and when to do things. This doesn't build trust or respect, some of the biggest things teenagers want from their parents.

### Authoritative

Authoritative parents tend to be less intense than authoritarian parents. While they have rules and set firm limits, they enforce them by explaining why those rules are in place and using positive reinforcements. However, authoritative parents always nurture and support their children regardless of how their child behaves.

Authoritative parents may tend to be too lenient. They set firm limits, but they sometimes fail to enforce them. They may be permissive to bad behavior and sometimes become somewhat neglectful as they overestimate the independence and self-discipline of their child.

Children raised under the authoritative parenting style will likely become healthily independent, successful, well-behaved, and self-disciplined. These parents raise their children to be confident and not blindly obedient but to act responsibly. This also means a child can have their say without it being the last word.

### Permissive

Permissive parents are on the opposite side of the parenting spectrum than authoritarian parents. Permissive parents avoid setting any limits or rules with their children for fear of upsetting them or stifling their "true nature." Children's bad behavior is often brushed off with phrases such as "kids will be kids."

Permissive parents try to be more of a friend to their children than a parent. They dismiss the idea of keeping their children under strict control. This means that children are not taught to have manners, be responsible, or follow a schedule. If the parents do try to discipline their children, it's often done with bribery.

Permissive parents are highly supportive and emotionally available. They are nurturing and warm and not demanding of their children. Children's ideas and thoughts are taken seriously, even if it means eating unhealthy food, staying up at all hours, or missing school.

These children grow up to be very self-confident and have good social skills; however, they are often demanding of their peers and act selfishly. They are not taught responsibility or respect.

### Uninvolved

This "parenting" style is sometimes called neglectful because these parents are unavailable to their children. They show little responsiveness to the needs of their children and rarely show any warmth or affection. Uninvolved parents are often so involved in their own lives and problems that they assign no time to their children.

These parents, like permissive parents, do not set limits or rules for their children and do not demand much from them. Uninvolved parenting does not refer to busy or "free-range" parents (which we will cover next). While it is not always intentional, uninvolved parents do not make themselves emotionally available to their children.

This parenting style often leads to inferior performance from their children in almost every aspect of life, including social competence, anxiety and stress, empathy, etc. For this reason, and for its failure to meet a child's needs, it is considered the worst parenting style.

### Free-Range

Free-range parenting focuses on allowing your child to face the natural consequences of their actions—as long as it is safe to do so. While free-range parenting is by no means neglectful, it offers children more freedom and responsibility to find their own feet and learn independence.

Free-range parents avoid over-protecting or allowing fear and worry to guide how they parent their children. They encourage their children to play in nature and observe the natural occurrences of life. They believe in building independence through less supervision, allowing their child more freedom to make their own decisions, and dealing with the consequences that come along.

Free-range parenting doesn't mean children are left without rules, boundaries, or limits. They are instead given the tools and taught the skills to make effective decisions for themselves.

A big question that is often brought up with free-range parenting is how old a child should be before they are allowed to be home alone. While opinions may differ, each state has its own laws regarding this decision. Be sure to do your research before approaching this method of parenting.

Some parents may think it is normal and expected for teenagers to be rebellious. They simply accept that this is a period in their lives when they are "difficult" and don't set any boundaries or address the consequences of their teenager's bad behavior.

Giving in like this removes any aspect of respect—both for parents and teenagers. Teenagers will see this as a sign of weakness. For a time, they will enjoy their freedom to do whatever they want. However, after a while, they may wonder if their parents are not enforcing rules because they no longer care about or love them. For example, these teenagers break curfew, but the parents don't seem to care. The teens may fail a grade, but parents don't say anything about it.

## THE 7-STEP PROCESS

In this book, I will lay out seven steps that can be implemented to parent your teenager effectively. These steps are:

1. Understand your teenager.
2. Communicate with your teenager.
3. Set boundaries for your teenager.
4. Build a lasting relationship with your teenager.
5. Give your teenager more responsibility.
6. Discipline your teenager.
7. Don't forget to take care of yourself.

# UNDERSTANDING YOUR TEEN

**Kendra's POV:**

There's an important exam tomorrow. Kendra has messed up and procrastinated, and now she has only a few hours to study. Kendra's best friend has just broken up with her boyfriend, and, as a good friend, she cannot realistically leave her friend to deal with this alone. She's currently trying to study between long and emotionally heavy texts from her friend. Last night, she went to bed at 2 a.m. because she just couldn't fall asleep. She's tired, overwhelmed, and emotionally charged.

**Kendra's Mother's POV:**

She walks into Kendra's room. Kendra's books are spread over the floor, but she is on her phone. This girl is trying to pull a fast one on her. She can tell when her daughter is just pretending to study.

"You're not going to get much studying done if you're on your phone the whole time," she says. Kendra sighs. (We know she is emotionally charged because of her friend's messages.) Kendra's mother mistakes this for attitude. "Give me your phone. It's the only way you'll get your studying done."

Now, Kendra's anxiety spikes. Not only is she attached to her phone, but her friend will have no one to talk to. Or worse, she will think Kendra is choosing to ignore her. Kendra shoves her phone into her mom's hand, and for the rest of the evening, she struggles to concentrate on her studying because she is worried about her friend and upset with her mother for taking her phone away.

**How could this situation have gone differently?**

First, Kendra's mother could have spent some time discussing boundaries with Kendra—making time for friends while prioritizing schoolwork.

Second, Kendra's mother could have taken a step back and allowed Kendra to be on her phone while studying. As a result, Kendra may have received a bad grade on the test because she did not study properly. This would be a direct consequence of her actions, for which Kendra would have to take responsibility. Taking Kendra's phone away was an unrelated punishment, as she might have mistaken it as punishment for being a good friend.

Third (and what this chapter will cover), Kendra's mother could have asked Kendra why her phone was so distracting. Kendra might have explained that her friend was having a difficult time, and her mom would understand that taking her phone away could only cause more stress.

## THEIR DEVELOPING BRAIN

When teenagers go through puberty, they deal with more than just physical changes. During this time, hormones begin those physical changes, but they also affect the brain in some interesting ways.

Hormones actually change the structure of the brain, altering the way the brain cells are organized and activated by stimuli. This affects how teenagers learn things, how they respond to situations, and how the brain continues to develop.

A significant change you may recognize in your teenager during this stage of life is their attention-seeking or reward-seeking behavior. Your teenagers could begin taking undue risks to get a reaction from you.

The adolescent brain has a way of learning that is different from adults and children. Teenagers learn by reinforcement. This means that teenagers will take risks in situations they have not encountered before; they will simply react. Then, they look for feedback. They see how you, as their parents, respond to this behavior and how their friends react.

If they receive positive feedback, this reinforces that the choice they made was the correct one. But if they receive negative feedback, they know their guess was wrong and will use that information to try and make a better guess next time. Teenagers learn better this way. Simply telling a teenager what the outcome will be is likely to have little to no effect. This is why it is so important to give your teenager the freedom to make decisions and the responsibility of dealing with the consequences.

Teenagers are wired to take more risks. They engage in risk-taking behavior because they seek that reward on the chance that they have done the right thing. As an adult, you may already know what the right thing is. But, as a teenager, they are still learning.

For instance, you have just caught your teenager smoking. You know this behavior is incorrect, and you let them know by grounding them, shouting at them, and taking away their cellphone. However, you have not seen the positive response your teenager received from their peers. Smoking gave them the reward of being accepted by their friends. Therefore, your teenager can take the harmful effects of smoking as an acceptable consequence of having their friends' approval.

Teens also use this method to develop their identity; they try different behaviors and ways of expressing themselves to see what gives them that reward and what sticks with who they truly are. If your teenager makes a change in appearance or wardrobe but doesn't receive the feedback they were hoping for, they will go back to their previous style or find a new one to try.

This is also why teenagers become so enraged when you don't allow them to take those risks and act in those attention-seeking ways. You are essentially taking away their learning opportunities. If you prohibit your child from expressing themselves the way they want to, you do more than stifle their self-discovery. You also remove their chance to try it out for a while and analyze the feedback they get from it, learning for themselves whether or not this behavior fits in with who they want to be.

## THEIR EMOTIONAL STATE

It is no surprise that teenagers can be rather moody. Their emotional state is notoriously fragile. One minute your teenager could be laughing and joking with you; the next, they are screaming at you and slamming their bedroom door.

I like to think of a teenager's emotional state like this: Your teenager has just been given a new horse, a prize stallion. But they have never ridden a horse, nor do they know how to. They get tossed onto this stallion's saddle and taken to a long winding road. The stallion takes off in a sprint, and the best your teenager can do is hold on for dear life and do what they can to stay in the saddle.

They have not yet learned how to control this stallion, calm it, read its signals and know what it wants, or make it stop.

So, you may think your teenager is overreactive, dramatic, or sensitive; but the truth is that they have not yet learned how to regulate and control their emotions. Sadness can feel like depression. Irritation can feel like rage. Confusion can feel like being completely lost and misunderstood. Attraction can feel like sexual desire.

Have you ever noticed how teenagers tend to react to temporary setbacks as if they are permanent? They have not yet learned how to remove themselves from a situation and analyze it. Teenagers can only focus on the here and the now. For all they know, *everything* is permanent.

Emotional changes that may occur during adolescence are:

- Your teenager may develop confidence issues, becoming more self-conscious and sensitive. It's common for teenagers to take a while to become comfortable in their skin. With things like acne, weight gain, voice cracking, etc., it is easy to become less confident or to be sensitive about commentary involving these changes.
- Because your teenager is discovering who they are, finding their identity, and going through all these changes, they may become less sure of themselves—not only in their physical appearance but also in their decision-making and personality. Your teenager may be unsure about who they are, what they want to be, what to study, what to wear, etc. Every decision becomes impossible to make. They are dealing with unfamiliar territory and can't be sure of anything.
- Your teenager may start struggling with conflicting thoughts. Surely you have experienced the feeling of not knowing quite where you stand with your teenager. Do they hate you? Are they okay? Should you leave them be? Teenagers may also be struggling to figure out how they feel. Part of them wants to love, appreciate,

and respect you because you are their parent. Another part of them is saying that you just don't understand them, you don't care. Not only this, but they have conflicting thoughts about what to do, how to behave, and how to feel.

- The friends in your teenager's life may also become more important to them during this time. Maintaining relationships with their peers is a priority for them. Their peers are who they will turn to, who they trust, and who they will listen to. Peer opinions are critical to them.

- Feelings toward your teenager's friends may include sexual feelings—attraction and desire. Puberty is when your teenager's body starts becoming sexually mature. Of course, we know puberty does not mean they are ready for sex, but it does mean that their brain will signal sexual desire and arousal. This can be overwhelming and confusing for a teenager to navigate.

- Because of all this self-consciousness, indecision, and rapidly changing moods, adolescence is a confusing time for your teenager. It may benefit both of you to recognize that not every emotion is a "true" emotion. It's easy to confuse anger with sadness or tiredness with anger. There's so much going on inside a teenager's head that it is understandable if they get it wrong now and then.

During their early adolescence, teenagers become hyper-sensitive to being admired and respected. All they want is to be accepted and feel like they belong and are valued. This does not only go for peers and friends. Teenagers crave acceptance and respect from their parents, teachers, and coaches. They want to get that feedback that they are doing well and behaving correctly.

This is more important than anything to them. They want to know that you, as their parents, value and respect them and that they belong in the family. Teenagers are often denied this because all parents can focus on is behavior and bad moods. Parents can so easily neglect all the achievements and successes, focusing instead on the mistakes and downfalls. Remember to make an effort to assure your teenager that you are proud of their accomplishments and love them unconditionally.

## DEVELOPMENT OF SELF-AWARENESS

Self-awareness can be described as one's ability to recognize their own actions, emotions, and thoughts and objectively analyze whether or not those emotions, actions, and thoughts align with their values or moral compass. This is a valuable skill to possess, as many of us are too emotion-driven or too personally attached to objectively analyze our behavior.

Self-awareness comes with many advantages:

- Knowing what you want out of a situation and knowing what type of person you want to be can help you make the right decisions. Self-awareness gives us the power to influence outcomes because we can behave according to our values and beliefs, which is more likely to result in favorable or pleasant outcomes.

- Self-awareness helps us to become more confident in our decision-making. Not only do we know what we want, but we are confident in making decisions that will lead to that outcome. This clarity is valuable when making difficult decisions.
- Self-awareness teaches us to take a step back from the situation and analyze it. Because self-aware people can look at their own decisions objectively, they can also look at and understand other perspectives. Self-aware people can look at a decision or situation from multiple perspectives and use that information to make a well-informed choice.
- Because self-awareness teaches us to look *objectively*, it frees us from biases and other assumptions that may influence us. We can remove those influences from the situation and make an objectively good decision rather than a decision that is good only for us.
- Being able to look at things objectively also helps us improve our relationships. We can remove the bias and emotional feedback and instead act to benefit the relationship as a whole rather than just one party.
- Self-awareness improves our ability to regulate and control our emotions. We can step back and analyze why we are feeling a certain way and whether or not that is our true emotion.
- Self-awareness, confidence, and clarity in any situation help lower our stress about certain situations and decision-making.
- Acting according to our moral compass and values will help us be more fulfilled, more confident, and all-

around happier with who we are and what we are doing.

Does self-awareness not sound like exactly what your teenager needs? Does it not sound like the perfect thing to help your teenager overcome uncertainty and self-consciousness? Self-awareness is something with which teenagers struggle. There is too much clouding their mind to effectively make decisions that align with their moral compass, not to mention that they are not entirely sure what their moral compass is yet. It's difficult to compare your decisions, actions, and emotions to a baseline you don't have yet.

But you can help your teenager gain more self-awareness. You can help your teenager achieve that self-confidence, clarity, and surety in their decisions.

The first step is encouraging your child to talk through their struggles. When your teenager faces a challenge, prompt them to speak out loud about the problem and why they are struggling. Talking to someone about a problem can encourage problem-solving and opening up about what you truly want from a situation.

The important thing with this is to ask and not tell. Ask them what they want, where they are struggling, and what they feel. And when they answer, listen to them; listen to what they are feeling. Do not tell them or think you know better. Let them get to the answer independently rather than pushing it onto them.

The second step is making sure your teenager is looking through a balanced perspective. If your teenager only points out the negatives and weaknesses, highlight the bright sides and strengths. If your teenager only mentions the positives and advantages, be sure to bring their attention to any potential pitfalls. This isn't to discourage them but simply to make sure they are making decisions with *all* the information at hand. Teenagers can be blind to certain aspects, and you can bring those aspects to light.

The third step is ensuring your teenager is acting on their own terms rather than in comparison to someone else. Make sure your teenager does not let someone else affect or influence their decision negatively. Do not let them compare themselves to siblings, cousins, friends, or classmates. A decision should never be made to outdo or become the same as someone else.

The most important thing in helping your teenager develop self-awareness is to give them the freedom, time, and space to figure it out for themselves. They are trying to learn *self*-awareness, not *parental*-awareness. Advise and guide them through the process, but do not take over.

Just as you don't want them to compare themselves to peers or siblings, you do not want them to compare themselves to you. To develop independence and identity, they must make decisions according to their *own* beliefs, morals, and desires.

This is where self-awareness is crucial for you, as a parent, to possess. You need to ensure you are not subconsciously influencing your teenager's decisions. Guide them correctly, and advise them when they ask for it, but you should let them form their own conclusion and act on their intuition.

Think of parenting your teenager this way: Your teenager is running on this stallion that they do not know how to control. You have long since learned how to manage your stallion. Parenting your teenager involves taking their hand and teaching them the methods to control the stallion and then letting them adjust those methods to what works for them and their stallion. It is NOT climbing onto their stallion yourself and turning it in a different direction. First, this will never teach your teenager control; second, your stallion and your teenager's stallion are entirely different. This means that your teenager's challenges will differ from those you have faced or will face.

Not teaching your teenager how to be independent is detrimental because, eventually, your teenager will grow up and move out. They will still not know how to control their stallion, and then they won't have you to do it for them anymore. It is much better to teach them while you are still there to help fix big mistakes, advise them through challenging times, or hold their hand when they are overwhelmed.

## HOW TEENS DEVELOP INDEPENDENCE

Being independent is something that everyone should learn, not just teenagers. It's vital for children to learn independence from their parents, those in relationships to learn independence from their partner, and friends to learn independence from their friend group.

Without autonomy, losing your sense of identity and self is easy. Independence doesn't only refer to doing things on your own but also to simply *existing* on your own terms and not in relation to someone else. It requires asking, "How do I do this on my own?" and, "Who am I without my parents, friends, or partner?"

For teenagers, learning to exist on their terms can be highly advantageous because it increases self-esteem and confidence. They can be assured of their abilities to make decisions and act of their own volition. It helps to stamp out some of that uncertainty and cloudiness when they can act on their own values and morals.

As teens learn to have more confidence and be more assured of themselves, they can handle external challenges better. Circumstances are less likely to debilitate and confuse them because they know they can get through any difficult patch.

Practicing independence also teaches your teenagers how to be self-reliant. Being dependent means that you can do it but don't. Reliance means that you are unable to do something. Teaching your teenager to do things for themselves and depend on themselves encourages them to learn how to do the things they need to get done. They must become self-reliant because they depend on themselves now.

For instance, if your child has always been very indecisive, giving them the independence to start making choices for themselves encourages them to learn how to be more decisive. They will soon recognize what a good decision looks like versus a poor decision. Their decision-making skills will improve and increase rapidly.

Allowing your teenager independence will allow them to find their place in life, where they belong. They can find their sense of importance. Allowing them the freedom to make decisions for themselves will guide them toward their purpose and passion.

Self-awareness and independence go hand-in-hand. The more you allow your teenager their autonomy, the stronger their self-awareness will become. They will need your guidance now and then, but advice should be asked for, and it should be minimal. Refrain from taking control of the situation, trying to correct, or reprimanding.

Independence also offers your teenager motivation. That passion and purpose will be their reasoning for doing things, becoming self-reliant, and making good decisions. They will act toward something for a purpose, not just to get it done. Independence helps to improve qualities like self-discipline, self-trust, patience, empathy, and cooperation skills.

Your teenager is more likely to find happiness if they are independent, for many reasons. First, they can be who they want to be with confidence and assurance. Second, they can make decisions that push them toward their goals and align with their moral compass. Third, they are better at controlling and regulating their emotions, meaning they can diffuse their sadness or anger more quickly.

Being able to act of your own volition and not having to rely on or depend on others for decision-making can take a great deal of stress off your shoulders. Things in life move more quickly and easily when you can control what happens and how you react to certain things. Being independent and confident allows us that freedom. It will do wonders for your teen and their future.

Your teenager may struggle with being heavily influenced by peers and society. Allowing your teenager to develop their independence helps prevent them from being caught up in the opinions of others. They can do things *they* want to do that are important to them without the influence of others. Being independent prompts your teenager to think honestly about why they are doing something and why they are thinking or feeling a certain way, encouraging personal growth.

### How to Help Your Teenager Develop Independence

The first step to teaching your child independence is to lay the foundation that, no matter what decision they make, you will always be there to support them and love them unconditionally. Teach them that their mistakes are not failures; they are part of the learning process and proof that they are trying. If your teenager is confident that nothing they can do will ever deny them your love, they will be more confident in making their choices.

The second step is respecting your teenager's emotions, opinions, and decisions. If you question your teenager's every move, one of two things could happen. They may stop letting you in on their life, or they may become less and less confident in their decision-making skills because, no matter what they do, Mom and Dad will not approve. Make your home a safe place for your teenager to express their opinions and make decisions without judgment.

Take the time to help your teenager develop their decision-making skills. Try giving them the freedom to make all sorts of decisions. Allow them to decide what's for dinner, what their bedtime is, or what their curfew is. They may surprise you. If they choose unwisely, help them discover a solution or better choice rather than telling them they are wrong. Starting with low-risk decisions (such as food preferences) can begin the process of making those decisions for themselves.

The same goes for practicing other forms of independence. Take the risk and step back from your teenager. Allow them to do things independently and figure things out for themselves. Offer them more responsibility in the household, which doesn't always mean adding more chores to their list. It may involve replacing everyday chores with more significant tasks, such as helping with dinner or packing away the groceries.

It's important to remember that not every wrong decision should be fixed. If your teenager decides that they want their bedtime to be midnight, allow them to go to bed at midnight. They will soon start feeling sluggish and exhausted. If your teenager chooses to go to a party over studying for a test, they have to deal with a bad grade. So long as it is safe to do so (it won't threaten your child's long-term well-being or safety), allow your teenager to see how their decisions come with consequences.

The final step of teaching your child independence is teaching them how to look after themselves. You may focus all your energy on making sure your teenager can make independent decisions, but they still don't know how to cook. Involve your teenager in essential tasks such as buying groceries, making dinner, cleaning the house, maintaining the home, and putting gas in the car. These are all things they will eventually have to do on their own. If you don't teach them, who will?

### How Much Independence Is TOO Much?

If you are truly worried about your teenager making the wrong decisions, set some family rules. We will talk later in this book about setting limits and boundaries for your teenagers, and that is because it gives your teenager a lighthouse to hold their decisions up against. They can make decisions based on those family rules and know it will likely be the right decision. These rules should be fair for everyone and crystal clear so that there is no room for misunderstandings.

As we discuss later in the book, you can give your teenager as much independence as possible as long as they abide by family rules and boundaries. Freedom comes along with responsibility, and responsibility involves respecting the laws of the household.

As they grow and become more independent, these boundaries might change. If they behave in violation of these boundaries, they lose a level of independence—the consequence of their actions that they must now face.

## CONSIDERATIONS

Can you recognize a time in the recent past when you may have misunderstood your teenager's motivations for doing something or their feelings about a situation?

Do you feel there is somewhere in your teenager's life where you can offer them more independence and freedom to make their own choices?

Have you made it clear to your teenager that you will love them and support them no matter their decisions?

# 3

# COMMUNICATING WITH YOUR TEEN

**Mason's Father's POV:**

Mason is growing up so fast. It feels like he was falling off the swing set at the park just yesterday, and today his rugby team won the match of the season. Mason's father feels like time is slipping from his fingers; he really should spend more time with Mason before it's too late. He has been meaning to fix up the old Cadillac in the garage. It would be a great thing to do with Mason—spend time together while teaching him how to repair and maintain his own car. That's a grand idea.

**Mason's POV:**

It's been such a long day. He should be studying for a test, but he feels that he has at least earned an afternoon nap. For now, though, he is just scrolling on his phone, talking to his girl-friend. Suddenly, his dad walks into the room.

"Come downstairs. I need your help fixing up the Cadillac," his father demands. *Now?* Mason thinks. *But I am already so tired. Couldn't he have asked on the weekend?*

"Dad," Mason groans, "I am really tired. I just want to chill."

We know that Mason's father was hoping for more quality time with his son. Mason's immediate rejection hurts him.

"Come downstairs. We're going to work on that car."

How could this situation have worked out differently?

Neither Mason nor Mason's father communicated effectively in this situation. Instead of telling Mason that he was hoping for quality time together and an opportunity to teach him valuable skills, Mason's father ordered him to come down and help fix the car. Rather than framing it as a bonding experience, he stated it as a chore or task.

Mason failed to communicate that he was only rejecting the invitation because he was tired from his rugby match, not because he didn't want to spend time with his father. If Mason had offered to help his father on the weekend, explaining that he didn't have the energy for manual labor at that time, his father might not have felt so rejected, and they could have agreed to spend the time together on the weekend.

By ordering Mason to help him fix the car, the whole purpose behind the task—bonding with and teaching Mason—has been negated because it is now a chore filled with tension and frustration from both parties.

## TEENAGE COLLOQUIALISMS

Does your teenager ever open their mouth and spew the most nonsensical sentences? Do you hear your teenager and their friends talking and honestly can't tell what's happening? Why are they using words that don't make sense?

This section goes hand-in-hand with understanding your teenager. It may be intimidating to talk to your teenager when you know they speak differently. What if they respond to you, and you have no idea what they are saying? That won't be a very communicative conversation. You're just going to stand there looking like an idiot. Or worse, what if they disrespect you and you are none the wiser?

You may be surprised to know that language is another way teenagers exercise independence and expression. Teenagers of each generation create a language that is just theirs; it belongs to no one else. They do this to feel that sense of independence and *apartness* from their parents.

Think of language and communication like fashion. It's a sense of expression, defining which generation you are a part of. Anybody still using "YOLO" is obviously not from this generation of teenagers, and anybody who is from this generation and uses the word "YOLO" is seen as uncool and an outcast. Just as our generation would not be caught dead wearing today's fashion, your teenager would be ridiculed for wearing your clothes.

Now, while the style may confuse you, you can often tell when someone is wearing a t-shirt and when they are wearing a dress. The same can't necessarily be said for language. You *might* be able to decipher a meaning based on contextual clues, but you can't be sure you've interpreted it correctly.

And it seems that just as you master the one generation's slang and can finally keep up, everything has changed, and now the language you understand is outdated and uncool.

Unfortunately, with language, your fears are correct; they *are* doing this to make sure you cannot understand. A primary function of creating this new language is to make sure that parents can't know what they are talking about. However, it is not as bad as you fear. They often use this language ironically, as a joke, because it makes them laugh. Being able to talk openly about things in front of someone who doesn't understand can be entertaining. It's only in rare cases that it is actually used to keep something from you. It's only when parents are doing things like listening in on conversations or reading through their texts that teenagers will lean into a language that their parents don't understand.

Below, I list 20 slang terms that the teenagers of this generation frequently use. The most important thing to note here is that you shouldn't be *using* this language. I offer up these explanations so that you may have a better idea of what your teenager is saying; so you can *understand your teenager*. If you attempt to use your teenager's language, much as if you tried to wear your teenager's clothes, you will receive a series of questioning glares.

## *Slang Terms Used by Teenagers of This Generation*

**AF**: As F*ck

**Body Count**: Asking or talking about someone's "body count" refers to how many sexual partners they have had. Unfortunately, girls are ridiculed for having a high body count, while boys are praised.

**Cheugy**: This term describes something outdated or no longer cool.

**Extra**: Refers to someone or something being over-the-top or too excessive. It may also be used as self-deprecating humor.

**Fam**: Refers to a group of friends.

**Flex**: This refers to when someone is showing off. A common phrase is, "Weird flex, but okay," which is often used to address when someone brings up something that is either nothing to "flex" about or irrelevant to the current conversation.

**I'm Finna**: Means "I am going to …" An example may be, "I'm *finna* dip," which means "I am going to leave."

**Karen**: Referring to someone as Karen means that they are entitled or acting rude. Karens are notoriously rude to those working in the service industry and often cause a big fuss over minor inconveniences. In short, you do not want to be referred to as a Karen.

**Lit or Fire**: Refers to something cool, trendy, or fun.

**LMIRL**: Let's Meet in Real Life.

**Lowkey or Highkey**: Lowkey refers to a little bit, and highkey refers to a lot. Lowkey may also refer to something on the down-low, while highkey would refer to something obvious or not hidden.

**Netflix and Chill**: This refers to when a couple plans to meet up and engage in sexual activities; this may range from making out to intercourse.

**No Cap**: This is used to confirm that someone is telling the truth; when someone isn't lying.

**Periodt**: This is used to conclude a statement by emphasizing it or solidifying it as fact.

**Salty**: This refers to when someone is upset, disgruntled, or jealous.

**Shook**: This is a synonym for "shocked" or "unsettled."

**Smash**: This term refers to casual sex. "I'd smash" is used to say, "I would have sex with that person."

**Snacc or Meal**: An attractive person may be referred to as a snacc. If they are exceptionally attractive, or if someone is trying to emphasize the compliment, they may refer to them as a meal.

**Spill or Sip the Tea**: Spilling the tea refers to sharing gossip or information. Sipping your tea means that you mind your own business. "The tea" refers to the information in question and can be used in other contexts; for example, "What's the tea?" would ask someone to share their information.

**Sus**: This term is short for suspicious or suspect and is used when someone is acting suspicious or a situation is questionable.

**Thirsty**: This refers to someone actively seeking attention from the sex they are attracted to, i.e., when a boy messages a girl or if a girl is trying to get the attention of an attractive boy.

**Turnt**: This is short for "turned up," which refers to becoming excited, getting high or drunk, or being in a very good mood.

## COMMUNICATING WITH TEENS

Let's consider the situation between Mason and his father once more. How do you think Mason would have reacted if, when his father asked for assistance on the car, he had said this instead: "Well done on the game today; I am so proud of you. I was wondering if you'd like to help work on the Cadillac this weekend. I think it's about time I showed you how to work on an engine."

If Mason had been prompted with good communication and given advanced notice about working on the car—rather than being ordered to drop what he was doing and work on it immediately—his response might have been, "Thanks, Dad. Sure, I am so tired from the game, but maybe we could start later after I've had a nap."

Much like adults, teenagers appreciate good communication. Consider being in your workplace and how your colleagues may communicate with you. Sure, the environment as a whole is more formal and professional, but there are basic communication rules that make any interaction—personal or formal—more pleasurable and more effective.

The first rule is to give advance notice. Even as adults, we get irritated when someone tries to pull us from something we are currently engaged in without prior notice. It's essential to offer our teenagers the same courtesy we would require.

When asking your teenager to do something in the house or for you, ask ahead of time and let them know that they can do it in ten minutes. You may need to remind them, but simply giving them those ten minutes to effectively transition to a new task will do wonders.

When you want to have a conversation with your teenager, consider that they may be busy with something already. I would not recommend giving too much notice to an important conversation without providing details. Telling your teenager that you want to talk without saying why may only cause them anxiety. Instead, before you sit down and get into a deep conversation, simply ask them, "Is this a good time to talk?" Doing this ensures that they can fully engage in the conversation.

The second rule is an oldie but a goodie: Remember that there is a time and a place. Paying attention to the environment and the timing of your communication with your teenager will play a significant role in how they respond. It's crucial to pick your moments well because you risk your teenager not paying attention or upsetting them unnecessarily if you choose the end of a long day at school or before a good lunch to have a serious conversation.

It's also important not to force the right environment. Sitting your teenager down and making it a huge deal will only make your teenager close up and go on the defensive. Simply keep an eye out for when both you and your teenager are not busy or stressed out.

The third rule is to remember that you should not lecture your teenager and give them no opportunity to participate in the conversation. I remember from my teenage years that every conversation I had with my parents until I was 19 would turn into a lecture on my behavior or what I would do in the future. Because of this, I would rarely talk to my parents about anything they could use as fuel to turn on a 20-slide presentation of how it would ruin my chances at a good life; this included most things.

The fourth rule is to avoid patronizing your teenager. The worst thing in the world is having to listen to and obey (with respect) someone talking down to you as if they think you are daft. Your teenager is sure to dismiss every word you say if it is clear that you do not trust them to make a good decision. By doing this, you cement the idea in your teenager's mind that, no matter what choice they make, they will be making the wrong one. Before offering advice, ask if your teenager needs it. Before offering to help, ask if your teenager needs it. Don't assume that they lack control of a situation.

The fifth rule is to listen to your teenager like you expect them to listen to you. Before offering advice and solutions, it's essential to hear them out. Instead of offering advice, ask what they plan to do. If you're unsure of something, ask questions. If your teenager feels heard, they are more likely to open up.

The sixth rule is to respect your teenager's point of view. Consider where they are coming from and how they may feel about something before asserting your ideas and opinions. While you might not agree with their perspective, or you might choose something else, it's necessary to show your teenager respect by hearing their views.

The seventh rule is to remain calm when talking to your teenager. Teenagers are always holding their breath for the moment when something they have said causes their parents to blow up in rage. Because of this, they often don't say anything at all. If you react explosively to your teenager, you will likely receive a similarly explosive response. You also inadvertently teach your teenager that reacting explosively to situations is okay. They may not say this, but they will see your behavior and copy it.

The eighth rule is not to take it personally when your teenager says or chooses to do certain things. Likely, your teenager is not doing something as a deliberate jab at you. When emotions run high (and teenagers' usually do), hurtful words can be thrown around without any weight, and unwise actions can be done without thought.

The ninth rule is not to force conversation. If your teenager expresses that they are unprepared for a discussion or do not want to talk to you about something, respect and accept that. You will never get open and effective communication out of your teenager if you force it. It is more likely that your teenager will dismiss and ignore you.

The tenth rule is never to assume you know the details and don't accuse your teenager. It's incredibly frustrating for anyone (not only teenagers) when a conversation is a one-sided attack on everything done wrong. Do not accuse your teenager of making bad decisions or assume you know why they made them. Instead, prompt them to analyze their choices by asking them what they might have expected the outcome to be.

The eleventh rule is to allow your teenager to think for themselves and develop their feelings and thoughts on a matter. Do not tell your teenager how to feel, think, or solve the problem in front of them. Offer them the independence to deal with a situation on their own terms. Allow your teenager the responsibility of solving their problems. As parents, we constantly run into the fray to "help" and "solve" everything for them. If you genuinely think your teenager cannot solve this complex problem alone, communicate your desire to help them and let them allow you in so you can solve it together.

And finally, the last rule is to remember and never compromise on your rules. By arguing your rules and allowing that line of conversation to be open, you suggest that your limits are negotiable. Instead, focus on the goal of the conversation and enforce the idea that, whether or not they agree with the rules, they are responsible for following them. Do not get drawn into a fight. For instance, when your teenager starts yelling at you, tell them that you can see they are angry and will wait until they have calmed down to continue having a civil conversation. Then leave the room and let them regulate their own temper.

## MINDING YOUR TONE

Perhaps I was wrong in saying that sticking to your rules was the final rule. The final rule deserves its own section due to its importance. Always be very mindful of your tone of voice.

You can tell a lot about how someone truly feels or thinks by how they choose to say something. Sarcasm is built on this fact. You may be speaking certain words, but how you say them might change their meaning altogether.

Humans are innately sensitive to picking up someone's tone of voice and identifying the emotions it might portray. This isn't any different for your teenager. They can recognize what your tone of voice gives away. You may say, "Oh, that's great, sweetheart," but your teenager can tell you were not paying attention to them.

While your tone of voice is important in every conversation, the one to be most wary of is the angry and aggressive tone that tends to show through when you're upset. How often do you yell at your teenager? How often is it effective?

I hate to break this to you, but yelling at your teenager is likely to have either no effect at all or a very negative effect.

- Yelling at your child whenever you're upset creates an environment where you must be shouting to be heard.

- Eventually, after years and years of hearing you screaming at them, your child is likely to become desensitized to your tantrums. If you've spent your child's whole life screaming until you were blue in the face about some spilled milk, it will mean nothing to them when you yell about catching them smoking.
- Research (Wang & Kenny, 2013) shows that yelling at your teenagers may be just as damaging as using aggressive discipline.
- Constantly yelling at your child may also harm their mental well-being. I speak from personal experience when I say that now in my adult life, I am extremely sensitive to someone raising their voice around me. I become defensive and feel like I have done something wrong, even if not directed at me.
- Yelling at your teenager is a form of verbal abuse, especially if it is done for every indiscretion. Yelling is a very aggressive and ineffective way of communicating that only stresses your teenager out and makes them feel attacked.
- As mentioned in the previous section, reacting so vehemently to all sorts of situations teaches teens that such behavior is okay. This will lead to them reacting explosively in response to your discipline, as well as with their peers, creating a very short-tempered person.

## "THEY JUST WON'T TALK TO ME"

Perhaps you have tried everything already. You've done the shouting and the calm and thoughtful approach. Nothing is working. Your teenager has created a fortress around themself, and you can't see any way to get through to them. You're worried that the further and further they push you away, the less likely you'll be to restore that relationship.

What do you do then?

The first and most important thing is to spend time with your teenager. Let them know they can hang out with you and be around you without you constantly vying for more information about their personal life. Let them know that even if they aren't in a good space to open up and share their feelings, you still love them and want to spend time with them.

I remember when I was a teenager, I avoided spending time with my parents because whenever there was a moment of peace and quiet, they would begin with the notorious "So …," and then the 21 questions would come. Don't ask; just *be* with them. Instead of prompting them to share, share what you did with your day or tell them you are happy to spend time with them. Don't lecture them. Don't moralize everything.

Next, become engaged in their life. As parents, we continuously ask to be kept informed of what's happening in our teenagers' lives, but we don't make an effort to be anything more than the keeper of the house in which they live. We ask how the game went rather than showing up to watch it. We ask how the test went but don't even know what subject the test was on. We ask how their friends are doing but can't even name them all. Learn what matters to your teenager—not by interrogating them, but by listening when they speak. Make it known that those things also matter to you: their music taste, hobbies, interests, favorite YouTube channels, etc.

The theme here is that talking is not the only important thing. Being there for them is. You shouldn't only *tell* your teenager that you care but *show* them. Do something special for them to show your support. It doesn't have to be their birthday for you to get them something nice. You could buy them something they need for school, their room, or self-care; and get them a good-quality one that will do the job right. They will appreciate the gesture as it shows that you listen when they speak.

You could also just have some fun with them. When they were younger, you would play games with them, have fun, and try to entertain them as often as possible. Why should that stop now that they're a teenager? Neither of you deserves to be having any less fun together. Take the time to find an activity you can do together, even if it's not one you would conventionally enjoy. The idea here is to enjoy your time with your teenager and get them to enjoy their time with you.

Try brainstorming some ideas for you to have fun together and stay open-minded. Sometimes the weirdest ideas can lead to the most fun; if they don't, they might lead to another good idea. Plan what and when to do this, and then be reliable and follow through.

If—and when—your teenager does decide to open up and share, don't butt in. Don't interrupt. Don't advise. Just listen. Sit back and appreciate that you have made a breakthrough. Listen to and validate their feelings, regardless of how *you* feel about the situation. Once they open up, do not harp on the small, unimportant things, like if they cuss while telling you a story.

Let them take the lead on where the conversation goes, what they choose to share with you, and what they decide not to. Don't force more information out of them. Don't turn the conversation serious. Don't make a big deal. Even though I am sure at this point you are secretly jumping for joy that you've finally broken through to your teenager, you need to act cool; this is not the time to be extra.

## CONSIDERATIONS

While reading this chapter, have you identified a moment when you may not have communicated in the best way with your teenager?

Can you think of ways to improve your communication with your teenager?

Did you recognize any of the teenager slang terms at the beginning of this chapter? Did learning the meaning of any of those terms unlock something about your teenager that you never understood before?

# 4

# SETTING BOUNDARIES FOR YOUR TEEN

Lauren was everything that her mother could have asked for in a daughter. She was intelligent, funny, strong-willed, and beautiful. Because Lauren's mother loved her so much, she allowed Lauren to have whatever she wanted. Even if ice cream in the freezer were meant for her father, Lauren would be allowed to have it. Even if the candy hidden in her mother's bedside drawer wasn't meant for Lauren, she'd be allowed to have it.

When Lauren went on playdates and would try to take toys from other children, her mother would tell the other child to learn how to share. When Lauren's father got Lego sets for his birthday, Lauren would be allowed to open the box and play with it if she wanted to.

Now, Lauren is 16 years old. She has never learned to respect people's personal belongings. Her mother and father have had to start hiding their money under their cars' seats, so Lauren doesn't take it. Lauren's father keeps his Lego sets at his brother's house because Lauren decided to take and sell three of his other builds. Lauren is constantly reprimanded at school for taking other students' belongings without permission.

And today, Lauren has been put in custody for shoplifting.

How could Lauren's parents have stopped this from happening?

Lauren's parents should have enforced boundaries, taught respect for someone's personal belongings, required asking permission before taking something, and expected respect when their answer was no. At this stage in life, it may be challenging to retrain Lauren to know that she cannot simply take what she wants without permission or consequences.

## DO TEENS REALLY NEED BOUNDARIES?

Does a tourist in a new country need road signs to know where they are going? Of course! The same applies to a teenager. Remember the stallion we spoke about earlier in this book? Remember the long road that your teenager is running down at full speed? Think of boundaries as fences your family has put up to ensure that your teenager's stallion does not steer them entirely off the course. The fences do not go down the whole road, but they protect your teenager from running head-first into ditches, thornbushes, and swampy waters.

When you were a teenager, flying down this road at top speed, you may or may not have had these guide rails in place. If you did, you know where they are and how to reinforce them for your child. If you didn't have the fences, you know what lies beyond them; you know you have to protect your child from that.

These fences are meant to be installed and reinforced for years before your child ever gets that stallion called puberty. Your teenager may not know the road, but they know those fences, and they know not to cross them.

This is what boundaries mean to a teenager. Boundaries act as a guide on where not to go or what not to do.

Boundaries are the beliefs that your family and household have about how to go about your lives; what behavior is encouraged, what is unacceptable, and what is right and what is wrong. Each family has its own set of boundaries and a way of enforcing them.

One family may allow their teenagers to date so long as they maintain their responsibilities at home and school, such as completing their chores and getting good grades. Another family may only allow their teenager to date after they reach fourteen years old. Another family may allow their teenager to date, but only after they have known the person for a specific time and have introduced them to the parents.

All boundaries can (and should) be adjusted to the values and beliefs of the family. When rules are created for your teenager, they need to be based on these boundaries to be truly effective and for your teenager to truly abide by them. However, one critical factor will determine whether or not your limits are effective. Boundaries should be in place for *everyone*. If you require your teen to knock before entering your room, you should also knock before entering theirs. If your eldest teenager was allowed to date at 14 years old, then your newly 14-year-old should also be offered the same courtesy.

Boundaries should be reasonable and fair, and part of that is ensuring everyone is on the same page. Bedtimes and dating will not apply to you as a parent, but respect, privacy, honesty, and communication will be just as crucial for you to live by as it is for your teenager. Each family member must know the boundaries and be able to hold themselves accountable and responsible for abiding by those boundaries.

The thing about boundaries is that they often come with rules. However, when limits are enforced correctly, rules can become redundant. If you have implemented the boundary of respect, you do not need the rule to ask permission before going out with friends.

Some boundaries are lifelong; the rules are implied, and even in adulthood, they should be followed, such as respect, abiding by the law, or privacy. But other boundaries suggest rules that must change as your child changes. For instance, you may have a boundary regarding internet safety:

- Your child may not have a phone until they are 12 years old.
- When your child is 12 years old, they can get a phone, but they may only have messaging applications on it, no social media.
- When your teenager turns 15, they may now have social media but must make their accounts private.

- When your teenager turns 17, you give them more freedom regarding their social media accounts, with the condition that you are following them and can see all the content they post.
- Eventually, when your teenager turns 18, you can lift all these restrictions and allow them to navigate the internet on their own. You can do this with the assurance that you have drilled internet safety into them, and they will continue to make decisions accordingly.

This is how rules can adjust while the overarching boundary—protect yourself on the internet—remains unchanged.

## WHAT TYPE OF BOUNDARIES DO THEY NEED?

Boundaries are created uniquely for every family. What may be important for you and your family may be less of a priority for another. What may be unimportant for you and your family may be a huge dealbreaker for another. Boundaries are created based on and surrounding the values and beliefs of your family, clarifying which behavior is acceptable and which is not.

The first step in developing boundaries for your teenager is talking to your spouse or partner, the person who will be helping you enforce those boundaries. This is a long conversation about what beliefs and values you would like to pass down to your children. What things are non-negotiable, and what other ones are you willing to let slide?

This is not when you will be discussing rules; remember that. Imagine the boundary is the fence you place along the wall; the rules you set within that boundary are how many rungs you put on the fence. It starts with five rungs (very high) so that your teenager cannot possibly get over it—strict rules.

Over the years, you can remove a rung because your teenager already knows not to cross the fence—adjusting or removing rules when appropriate for their age. Eventually, if you have done it right, you won't need any rungs; just two posts to mark where that boundary is, reminding your child of the danger beyond. But no rungs are necessary because it is well-established in their mind not to cross that boundary.

During the conversation about setting boundaries, it's about identifying the big themes you want to instill in your child, such as respect, kindness, faith, etc. Have an open discussion with your partner about what your child needs to learn as they grow up.

Consider these questions when having this conversation:

- What boundaries take the highest priority?
- Which of your boundaries are—and are not—negotiable?
- What related consequences can we use to enforce these boundaries?
- Will these boundaries be adjusted or removed as your teenager grows up?

## HOW TO SET BOUNDARIES

So you have spent the time with your partner to narrow down exactly what boundaries you'd like to set for your children. Now, it's time to set them. But how do you do that?

### *Timing Matters*

Timing is a critical factor when setting boundaries. It would be best to choose a time when you and your teenager are relaxed, calm, and available to talk. You do not want this conversation to be rushed or not addressed with the proper amount of care and caution. Choose a moment when there will be no rush and enough time to go into as much detail as necessary. It's also important to leave time after the conversation—time for you and your teenager to unwind and relax after an intense discussion.

Furthermore, the last thing you want to do is have this conversation when you are upset and angry or when your teenager is upset or feeling vulnerable. If you choose to have this conversation when either of you is not in the right mindset, it can lead to more harm than good. If you choose a moment when your teenager feels particularly vulnerable, this conversation may be too much for them to deal with mentally. If you choose a moment when you are particularly angry or irritable, your teenager will see these boundaries as a punishment.

### Remember, Tone Matters

Yes, this is a very serious conversation, but that doesn't mean it needs to be dull, intense, or humorless. Remember that we spoke about how important our tone of voice is when speaking? This conversation is no different. You can be saying the most gentle and caring words, but if your tone of voice is aggressive or unhappy, your teenager will pick up on that.

The best tone to use when discussing boundaries is friendly and casual, without downplaying the seriousness of the topic. Be firm in your limitations, letting your child know which boundaries are non-negotiable and on which ones they can ask for fair adjustments. Let your teenager know *why* these boundaries are being put in place; make it clear that they are not punishments and are being put in place to keep them safe and healthy.

### Include Your Teenager in the Conversation

That sounds obvious, but it can be easy to forget that this shouldn't be a one-sided conversation. It's essential to allow space for your teenager to ask questions, to clarify or elaborate on things. If your boundary is non-negotiable, listen to their concerns, consider them, but be firm that this boundary is mandatory. If the limitation is open for negotiation, let your teenager know, and then listen and respond to their feedback.

Your teenager is much more likely to agree and abide by these boundaries if they view them as fair and reasonable because they were included in creating them.

*Negotiating*

Negotiating does **NOT** mean

- You should shoot down all of your teenager's concerns and ideas.
- You should accept every one of your teenager's counterpoints.

Negotiating is where you and your teenager reach a healthy and fair middle ground. If your teenager disagrees with a boundary, and you are willing to negotiate, then be open to adjusting the limit according to their needs without overstepping the reason for the limitation in the first place.

If your teenager is expecting too much of a change to the boundary, let them know that you are willing to revisit the discussion after some time has passed and they have proven that they are responsible enough for the limit to be adjusted.

Do not let your teenager negotiate on non-negotiable boundaries. Don't allow the conversation to continue, but don't be aggressive. Calmly tell them they can negotiate on the other boundaries, but this one is not up for debate.

*Clear and Concise*

When laying out the boundaries, do not confuse your teenager with other small talk or unnecessary explanations. Keep the description of the boundaries clear and concise so there is no room for miscommunication or misunderstandings. Explain the limit clearly, and then encourage your teenager to ask about anything they aren't sure about.

**Tip**: Do not use phrases like "Do you have any questions?" or "Do you understand?" Teenagers may not feel comfortable bringing up questions, even if they have them. Instead, say, "Okay, ask me your questions now," or "I am ready to answer any questions now." This lets them know that you expect them to have questions and are ready to answer them.

### Rights vs. Privileges

Everybody has the right to shelter, food, clothing, and cleanliness. These are not things that should ever be withheld from your children as a consequence of not respecting a boundary. These are the things that your child is entitled to and to which they should always have access. Never should your child be denied their home, a meal, clothing, or a bath.

However, there are things your child has access to that are optional. Things like a car, television, cell phone, or being allowed to go out with friends are privileges you allow your child. These things can be denied from them as a consequence of disrespecting a boundary.

The key here is to ensure that only a relevant privilege related to the boundary is used as a consequence. It doesn't make sense to take away your teenager's cell phone because they were driving irresponsibly.

*Boundaries Exist to Keep Them Safe*

It is essential to let your teenager know that these boundaries are not meant as punishment. Let it be known that you have put these boundaries in place because you care about their safety, health, and mental well-being. Explain how not having these boundaries in place could negatively affect them.

*Be Clear About the Consequences*

Make sure your teenager knows what will happen if they step over a boundary. Simply saying that there will be consequences might not mean anything to them.

Lay out the consequences of breaking these boundaries for each instance. Clarify that if they break the boundary of prioritizing responsibilities over their social life, like ignoring their homework for a party, they will be grounded for some time. Tell them that if they stay up late watching television, it will be removed from their room.

Be clear. Be specific.

*Implement the Consequences*

You've had the conversation with them. They know the boundaries. Now you're done, Right? Wrong.

Now it's time to follow through with the consequences. In the ideal world, your teenager will abide by and live within the boundaries you have put in place. However, teenagers very seldomly behave in an ideal manner. Expect that they will push, cross, or even forget the boundaries. Be ready for it.

If it is safe to do so, allow the natural consequences of their actions to teach them why they shouldn't cross the boundaries; bad grades from not studying or exhaustion from staying up late. However, some consequences may threaten your teenager's safety, health, or well-being. This is when you should intervene and assist them in cleaning up the mess of breaking that boundary.

However, if the natural consequences are unsafe, or if there is little to no consequence for your teenager breaking a boundary, that is when you should implement the consequences you laid out for them. Take away their phone. Take the television out of their room. Ground them.

Be fair and reasonable. But do not let your teenager see that crossing the boundaries doesn't result in any pushback from your side. They will only take this as permission to continuously break that boundary to the point where it is no longer effective.

Include them in the setting of boundaries and in choosing what the consequences might be. You may be surprised that teenagers can be quite hard on themselves, perhaps suggesting a consequence that you would have deemed too harsh. Remember, teenagers are more likely to accept the consequences of crossing a boundary when they feel included. They are less likely to argue the fairness of a limit they themselves helped create.

## Be the Example

If you have set boundaries about driving safely and abiding by the rules of the road, you cannot be speeding, doing illegal merges, or forgetting to use your indicator. If you have set boundaries about prioritizing responsibilities, you cannot spend the whole Saturday watching Netflix while the kitchen remains in a state.

Show your teenager that you can live a full lifestyle within the boundaries you have set up. Show them what it means to live within the limits you are setting.

## TEACHING TEENS TO SET BOUNDARIES

Boundaries are more than just following a moral code and living according to beliefs and values. Boundaries are also about maintaining healthy relationships and a healthy balance to positively affect our mental well-being.

We must also teach our teenagers how to set healthy boundaries for themselves. Sure, we can teach them to abide by the limitations we set for them, but how can we be sure that they are maintaining their own healthy boundaries if we don't teach them what those might look like?

Your teenager may be respectful, not invade people's privacy, drive safely, and go to bed on time, but they also let their friends walk all over them. They believe they are obligated to be available to their friends at any hour. They might allow their friends to discourage and offend their faith. They may not know that this behavior is unacceptable.

The first step is teaching your teenager exactly what an emotional boundary is. An emotional boundary is a boundary we set to prevent others from hurting, using, or manipulating us. Setting emotional boundaries is *not* selfish. It is an excellent way to look after yourself and ensure you are not taken advantage of.

It is important to teach your teenager that setting these boundaries does not entitle them to attack, blame, and react aggressively to anyone who pushes them. Teach your teenager that when these boundaries are in place, they are responsible for how they respond to those who push their limits. They should not lash out and attack.

Instead, if someone starts disrespecting their boundaries, they should calmly let the person know what they are doing is unacceptable and kindly ask them to stop that behavior. This holds the person responsible for their actions and puts the ball in their court to change their behavior.

However, your teenager may not know how to recognize when someone is acting unacceptably. You may be able to prompt your teenager by asking questions such as, "You don't have to say any names, but do you have friends that you are sometimes uncomfortable being around?" or "Let's make a list of five things you would like your friends to stop doing."

By doing this, you urge your child to look at their friendships more analytically and identify behavior they deem unacceptable. Once they have identified the intolerable behavior, teach them to communicate their boundaries and ask their friends to modify their behavior.

You won't always have to do this. Once your teenager can start identifying these behaviors for themselves, they will be able to enforce their own boundaries effectively.

However, your teenager might still have problems. I found it very difficult to set boundaries for myself, as I thought it was easier and would cause less conflict if I just said yes to everything. It would help to let your teenager know the risks of not setting emotional boundaries. Teach your teenager that someone who pushes their boundaries does not respect them. Teach your teenager that if they expect others to honor their limits, they need to honor others' boundaries in return.

Beyond that, setting boundaries can be very intimidating. What if their friends reject them? What if they start feeling guilty about setting that boundary? What if it causes conflict? All of this can dissuade your teenager from wanting to set those boundaries at all.

This is where you, as their parents, should encourage them to take those baby steps; practice making small boundaries. Practice enforcing those boundaries by saying no and explaining why that behavior is not okay. Practice *not* having to defend boundaries for people to respect them. Once they have mastered enforcing those small boundaries, encourage them to set more significant boundaries.

If your teenager doesn't know how to enforce those boundaries or what to say when someone pushes back, give them the vocabulary. Having the right words in the arsenal for when it's needed can give your teenager the added confidence to speak up when they are uncomfortable.

- No, thank you.
- I am not comfortable doing that.
- Let me think about it.
- I'll have to ask my parents.

However, it's helpful to put yourself into your teenager's shoes. It's much easier to practice saying these things in the mirror than it is to stand up to your peers. If they are *still* uncomfortable or unwilling to enforce their boundaries, teach them to deflect or change the topic. Until they are comfortable enforcing their limits, they need to be able to get themselves away from the uncomfortable situation.

If your teenager is being offered a cigarette and is worried that saying no will cause conflict, they can say, "Oh, I can't. I tried it once and nearly coughed up a lung," or "I actually have to get going. My mom will kill me if I don't finish this assignment."

And last, perhaps one of the most important things in this section: digital boundaries. It is critically important to let your child know that digital limitations exist and are just as important. Being on the phone or behind a laptop screen offers the user a lot of anonymity. It can feel like what you do and say online isn't real and won't have consequences. Unfortunately, what happens online often does not have very tangible results.

However, things done or said online have the same emotional impact as things that happen in real life. Pointing at a girl and calling her fat hurts just the same way as posting an image of her and commenting that she has gained weight. It may hurt more because those words will stay there forever. Things that happen online are just as serious and real as what happens in real life. A screen does not make it okay.

Digital boundaries are crucial today, where technology is ever-prominent in our children's lives. Your teenager needs to know that anything they wouldn't do, say, or accept in real life does not have to be and should not be done, said, or accepted online either.

If your teenager would not get naked in front of someone, they shouldn't send nudes. If your teenager would not bully someone to their face, they shouldn't make rude comments online. If your teenager would not allow someone to touch or kiss them in real life, they should not allow that person to sext them.

## CONSIDERATIONS

What boundaries have you set with your teenager? What limits have you not yet set but are essential to set as soon as possible?

Do you think healthy and reasonable boundaries are in place in your home? Should some of these boundaries be removed? Should more limitations be implemented?

What are the consequences of not complying with boundaries?

Have you involved your teenager in the setting of boundaries and consequences?

Can you identify an area in your teenager's life where they have not effectively enforced their emotional boundaries? How do you think you can help them do so?

# 5

## BUILDING A LASTING RELATIONSHIP

When Jacob was a teenager, his parents expected a lot. They expected Jacob to bring home the best grades, sports awards, friends, a stable girlfriend, and still have time to care for himself.

On the weekends, he was expected to help them in the house, learning how to clean, repair, and maintain a home. His parents taught him everything there was to learn. He met all their high expectations because they taught him how to manage his time. They taught him how to treat her right and maintain a healthy relationship, so he married the girlfriend he had in school and is still in a stable and healthy relationship with her.

Jacob has a job now; he knows how to invest and save his money. He is in an excellent mental state because his parents taught him how to care for himself amidst a stressful and busy schedule. He is doing very well for himself. His parents did their best to give him a good life, and now he has one.

But he and his parents rarely ever talk to each other. They were great parents, but the truth is that much of their love was given through advice and lessons. Jacob can't remember the last time he was hugged and congratulated. He can't remember a time when he sat down and spoke to his parents about something other than how to improve and achieve.

Every conversation was a serious one. Sure, his parents were glad he had friends, but he couldn't recall if they remembered any of their names. He and his parents simply did not share those personal feelings. They were aware of his stress but not of his intense loneliness. They were mindful of the pressure on his shoulders but not the happiness he felt when they displayed his award in the dining room.

How could this situation have gone differently?

Jacob's parents were very concerned about Jacob's success. They did incredibly well teaching him independence, responsibilities, boundaries, and a healthy life balance. But they forgot to love their son just for being their son. They forgot the bond between parent and child as he grew older. They were so focused on the teenager that they forgot about the little boy and the man he would become.

Sure, their son is successful, but they are not around to see it because they allowed that relationship to come apart at the seams.

## WHY YOUR RELATIONSHIP WITH YOUR TEEN MATTERS

It's easy to think that teenagers need less of our time and attention than when they were little. After all, we are teaching them independence. That means we step back and let them be. This couldn't be farther from the truth. Our teenagers are in *more* need of our time and attention, not less. But they are sure as hell not going to express that. They aren't going to ask us or let us know they need more of our time.

Perhaps it won't be hours of playing in the park, and they may not ask us to admire every single doodle they make. The time will more likely be spent just listening to them, giving them our attention, offering a shoulder to cry on, or some words of wisdom. This shift is usually how the relationship between you and your teenager becomes severed: You stop giving them your time. You assume they don't need it or want it anymore. But they do. They want your love, and they need it.

The truth is that your teenager needs someone's love, affection, attention, and time. They crave it. If they do not get it from you as their parent, they will seek it out elsewhere. This could lead to a beautiful, healthy friendship where they lean on and support each other. It could lead to a fantastic relationship with their soulmate. Or it could lead to an unhealthy attachment style to someone who gives them the wrong type of attention. It could lead to your teenager seeking attention wherever possible, even if it's risky.

Do not pull away from your teenager at this time. Do not be overbearing or force yourself into their space and their lives. Just be there for them. Don't avoid them. Listen to them and be responsive to their needs. Don't advise when they need to vent. Don't keep quiet when they ask for an opinion. They want a relationship with you, but you often must make the first offer.

It's important to note that even if you are closer than you have ever been to your teenager, this does not guarantee that you will always agree. In fact, I can almost guarantee that you will have different opinions about multiple situations. Having a great relationship with your teenager will not make every day easy. There will still be hard days, days when you disagree, and days when you are both frustrating the other. This is normal. It happens in all relationships.

But a strong and healthy relationship ensures that not *every* day is terrible. You are not *constantly* disagreeing and driving each other loopy. A strong bond ensures that the heated argument in the kitchen doesn't lead to months of resentment and negative feelings. A healthy relationship means that both you and your teen can more easily and quickly find a solution or compromise to whatever disagreement is standing between you.

The last point, which is a bonus and not the main reason we try to cultivate a strong relationship with our children, is that they are more likely to listen to us. If we have a strong relationship with our teenagers, our opinion, advice, and input are more likely to influence their decisions.

As I mentioned above, this is not the only goal for building this relationship. Our goal is not to create a strong bond simply to influence our teenagers. However, this is something that will naturally happen.

Think about it; your teenagers are highly influenced by their peers and friends. This is because they are forming closer bonds with their friends; they are interested in what their friends think and feel about how they act. By continuing to keep the bond between you and your child strong and healthy, they will be concerned about what *you* think and feel about their behavior.

Beyond this, having a solid relationship will help you and your teenager to be on the same page about things. You can share your opinions and show mutual interest in each other's lives. You will know more about and be more involved in their lives, and you can be there for them when they need you—to talk, be a safe space for them, or take authority when their health and safety are at risk.

## HOW TO BUILD A STRONGER RELATIONSHIP

### *Spend Time Together*

*Periodt.* The first and most crucial step in building that relationship with your teenager is just spending time with them. This doesn't have to be a *thing*. Spending time in the park is just as good as hanging out in the living room.

A teenager may be skeptical about spending too much time with you, as it becomes less *cool* to hang out with your parents the older you get. But, once again, it doesn't have to be a thing.

If you have a home office, put your teenager's homework desk and setup in there. You'll be spending tons of time together.

Parallel play is a fantastic option for teenagers as it allows them to spend time with you without being too obvious about it. Let them cut the vegetables while you work on the pasta sauce. Let them water the garden while you repot some plants. Let them scroll on their phone while you watch a movie.

Remember not to ruin that quality time by nagging them, commenting on insignificant details, or trying to lure them into a deep conversation at every turn. Let them scroll on their phone. Let them slouch a little bit. Don't yell at them for letting out an accidental cuss word. Cherish those moments with them.

A conversation is bound to come about naturally, and *BOOM*, you are spending quality time with your teenager.

### Take the Lead

As I said, it will most likely be you who has to hold out the hand. It will be you who initiates conversation or suggests family time or activities. Your teenager might be *too cool* to express that they want to spend time together openly.

Don't be afraid to invite them to the garden, a spa, some shops, or around the block for a walk. Lead by example, prioritizing your relationship. If your teenager sees that you are making an effort to strengthen and build the relationship, if they see that you are not pulling away or leaving them on their own, they will soon start to follow your lead.

They might ask to sit by you while they do homework. They might offer to go to the mall with you. They might suggest a walk around the block. If you show your teenager that your relationship with them is very important to you, it will become essential to them too.

### Show Them You Care

Do you only ever praise and spoil your child when it's their birthday, Christmas, or they have made a significant achievement? When was the last time you got or did something for them just because? Do you ever purchase something, not because they needed something or deserved a reward, but because you love them?

If your teenager is having a stressful day and opens up their lunchbox to find their favorite snack with a scribbled heart on the packaging from you, it is bound to lighten up their entire mood. If your teenager is studying for a test and you bring them a plate of cookies to motivate them, they will remember that and love you for it.

Make an effort to show your teenager that you care. Listen when they speak and show that you pay attention to what is important to them. You don't have to break the bank to show someone you care. Putting a fresh towel in the bathroom for them before their shower is a sign of love. Doing their chores for them, just so they can have the night off, is a sign of love.

Never let your teenager forget that you love them with all your heart and soul. It may seem obvious that you do, but your actions will only strengthen and confirm that bond.

### Share Their Interests

Another way to show you care is to show an interest in the things that interest your teenager. Sure, you are probably not into video gaming, reading classics, or intense makeup routines. But if your teenager shows an interest in something, it will mean the world to them if you were to share that interest.

Nothing is more demotivating as a teenager than finding something that *finally* suits your personality and fits in with who you want to be, but your parent despises it or can't be bothered.

If you try to show an interest in your teenager's interests, you never know what you may learn—about yourself, about your teenager, or about something new that you never had an interest in before. Perhaps you spent your whole life thinking you were not creative or imaginative, but then your teenager asks to go to a sculpting class. You offer to take them and decide to go with them and see what it's all about. Suddenly, all that hidden creative potential morphs into a hobby the two of you can spend hours doing together.

Even if it does not interest you, make an effort for your teenager. They will appreciate the show of love, even if they can see you are bored out of your mind. It shows them that you are willing to discover new and crazy things if it means that they are happy.

## Don't Be Pedantic

Have you ever been watching a movie where the main character is so involved in the details of a project that they make very little progress with the overall goal? Have you ever seen how someone is so *zoomed in* on one aspect of a painting while the rest of the canvas is empty?

Has this ever happened in real life? Where you are doing something—and succeeding—and suddenly something ruins it? Don't record-scratch the moments you get with your teenager.

With adolescents, it's so important to choose your battles. Sure, if your teenager has disrespected you or your partner or has been aggressive with a sibling, there should be consequences. But is a little bit too much black eyeliner really the hill you want to die on? Is cutting their hair short detrimental to their safety, health, or well-being?

If you flip your lid about every slight discrepancy or choice they make that isn't aligned with what you would have done, you can't expect your teenager to be engaged and interested in a relationship with you. You wouldn't want to be surrounded by someone who questions and ridicules your every move.

Let your teenager be. If they respect the boundaries you have set in place and are safe and healthy, then just let them be. Having those boundaries in place will be a helping hand when building a solid relationship. You both know what is expected from the relationship. You know when to intervene and when to let it go.

It's also important to show them a little mercy sometimes. A little grace will go a long way for your teenager. Your teenager will remember the time you let them get off with something that should have resulted in negative consequences. If it's a common misdemeanor, then this grace is perhaps undeserved. But if it was a momentary lapse of judgment, a little grace goes a long way.

### Don't Be Toxic

I'll keep this one short and simple. Do not belittle your teenager. Do not be condescending to them. Don't humiliate or manipulate them. Do not normalize toxic behavior in a relationship that is meant to be healthy. You will not only lose the respect of your teenager, but you will also lose their trust.

## CONSIDERATIONS

Have you spent time with your teenager recently? Is there a way you can spend some more quality time with them soon?

When was the last time you showed your teenager a random act of kindness? When was the last time you showed them that you are interested in their lives and that you care about them?

What is an interest of theirs that you can start becoming more involved in? Is there a way for you to share that interest with them?

# 6

# GIVING YOUR TEEN MORE RESPONSIBILITY

When Jenna was a child, up until she was nineteen years old, her father did everything for her. He would make her appointments, drive her to school, help her with every one of her school assignments, buy her toiletries, help her budget, and cook all her meals.

Jenna enjoyed this. She barely had to lift a finger, and her dad was always there when she needed him, and she needed him a lot. Sure, she wanted to do things herself sometimes, but she knew it made her dad happy to help. He was a fantastic dad.

Jenna didn't bother getting her driver's license. Jenna didn't bother getting any summertime jobs. Whenever she wanted something, her father would get it or do it for her.

When she was nineteen years old and out of school, she wanted her own apartment on the other side of town. As always, her dad arranged it for her. He looked at apartments, checked the rent prices, looked for water or electrical problems, and soon found the perfect place for her.

She eagerly moved into her new place, on her own for the first time. Her first night there was a disaster.

Her dad had helped her to set up everything. Her laptop, Wi-Fi, television, and alarm system were all in place. Her furniture was assembled. Her kitchen stuff was packed away. Her fridge was stocked. He had even paid the first three months' rent so she would have time to get on her feet. She was good to go, so her dad went on his way across town.

But on the first night, when it came time for dinner, Jenna was stumped. She'd never made food for herself before and didn't know how. She stared at her fridge with anxiety for thirty minutes before deciding that it might be best to order in, at least for the first night. Eventually, she would learn how to cook, she was sure. That's what YouTube is for, right?

She reached for her phone. She found the number for the McDonald's down the street. And then she was struck with panic. She'd never ordered her own food before. She didn't even know what to say, let alone what to order for herself. What was it that her dad always chose for her? How did he greet the guy on the phone?

With a trembling hand, she put the phone back down. On second thought, she wasn't all that hungry after all.

Her dad called the next day. She sounded happy and enthusiastic; she was too embarrassed to confess the panic she had suffered the night before. Each day he called her, and each day she seemed less and less excited. He'd ask if she was okay, but she only said she wasn't feeling well.

Jenna had barely eaten in four days. She had tried to learn how to cook but didn't know how to work the oven. She didn't know what the lady on her phone meant when she said to "fry it to a golden brown." The few times she tried to cook, it hadn't ended well. She was starving.

Her dad suggested she see a doctor. He'd be able to come by on the weekend and help her do some meal prep for the next week. She agreed and hung up the phone, only to remember that she had never booked a doctor's appointment for herself. She didn't even know who her doctor was.

How could this situation have been different?

Jenna's father was great for always being ready to lend a hand when Jenna needed it. But he did her a great disservice by not handing over some responsibility as she grew up. He sheltered Jenna from the real world of having to look after herself. She depended on him for everything because he never taught her any better.

If Jenna's father had eased Jenna into responsibility by teaching her to drive, getting her a job, allowing her to order her food, or involving her in maintaining and upkeep of the household, then Jenna would have been better prepared for life on her own.

## WHY DOES RESPONSIBILITY MATTER

- It's incredibly unfair to expect someone to excel, or even be average, at something they have never before done. You can't expect your teenager to be responsible if you have not given them a chance to practice responsibility.
- With a well-established sense of responsibility, your child is much more likely to succeed in life, school, work, and society. Having a sense of responsibility means they will more easily focus on and complete tasks. They will be able to manage a balanced lifestyle.
- Responsibility and reliability often go hand-in-hand. Responsible people are reliable, and to be reliable, you must be responsible. Reliability is doing whatever it is that you have said you will do. Reliability is following through, following your words with actions. Responsible people do this well.
- Because responsible people are reliable, they are also trustworthy. You can count on the words of a responsible person. You can trust that they will follow through on what they say. You can trust that they will behave and act responsibly.
- Responsibility is about:

  - **Being Believable:** People can believe and trust what you say because it is true.
  - **Being Honorable:** You stick to your word, agreements, and promises.

- **Being Accountable:** You are persistent in handling things that are your responsibility, such as chores or homework.
- **Practicing Mutuality:** Doing for others as they would do for you.
- **Being Available:** You can openly discuss concerns or areas of confusion.
- **Being Civil:** You do not act with rudeness or meanness but instead with courtesy and kindness.

- Responsible people grow and develop more skills because they take accountability for their mistakes. Responsible people own up to their mistakes and are willing to face the consequences and improve themselves.
- Responsible people can act with more confidence. They know what they have to do and how to do it.

Teaching your child how to be responsible now, when their responsibilities are minimal, will set them up for success in the long term when they are in the world on their own. As a parent, you are not oblivious to the fact that an adult's responsibilities can be overwhelming and many. Teaching your children how to act responsibly now will allow them to face all of their adult responsibilities with more knowledge, more confidence, and less anxiety.

## GIVING YOUR TEEN MORE RESPONSIBILITY

### *Yes, No, Maybe*

When asking yourself whether or not to shift a specific responsibility over to your teenager, there are three answers: yes, no, or maybe.

To say **yes**, you must feel your teenager is ready for that responsibility. You must think that it is a responsibility they can successfully take on. It should be something that they can start making their own decisions about. Most importantly, *you* must be ready to accept your child's decisions. Keep in mind that by saying yes, you have agreed that it is okay for your child to walk home alone, wake up when they want, or get their own ride to a sport session.

By handing over the responsibility, you are also handing off the control. It is now in your teenager's hands; you expect them to take on the responsibility, and they expect you to trust them.

For example, let's say you have given your teenager the responsibility of looking after the family cat. This means you should trust your teenager to feed the cat, change the litter box, and brush through the cat's hair. It does not mean you should constantly check on the cat, its food bowl, and its litterbox. It does not mean you should always remind them to do their tasks. Sure, you may have to check and remind them at the beginning, as they get used to the new responsibility. But then you need to trust them to have it handled.

To say **no**, you must feel your teenager is not yet ready for this responsibility. Perhaps it is not yet legal for your teenager to start making that kind of decision for themselves. Maybe it is a responsibility where a mistake would significantly affect them or the family.

How you choose to say no, though, is very important. It's essential to be delicate about denying your teenager a responsibility. Rather than just saying no outright, explain to them why they cannot be given that responsibility for the time being.

Sometimes, however, the answer is **maybe**. These are opportunities when your teenager can negotiate a yes out of you. It is when the chances of your teenager gaining responsibility over something depend on their behavior. It may be something where they must first prove they can handle the commitment before you hand it off to them.

### Are They Ready?

To determine whether or not your teenager is ready for more responsibility, you need to assess

- **Their Maturity:** Your 14-year-old may be more mature than your 18-year-old. Teenagers mature at different rates; their maturity is a big indicator of what they can handle. Consider whether your teenager is mature enough and has the necessary skills for the responsibility you would like to give them.
- **Their Experience:** Has your teenager ever handled something similar to this responsibility before? How

did they take it? Your teenager must be allowed to find solutions independently. So, if it is responsible on your part to allow them the experience, then do so.

- **The Legality:** Consider whether or not it is legal for the responsibility to fall onto your teenager. There are laws about when teenagers may decide to leave home, leave school, consent, drink, etc.
- **Family Values:** Handing responsibility to your teenager is accepting that they may make decisions that do not match the family values. Of course, we hope that we have taught them correctly and that they will only do what we would, but this is not always realistic.

### Practicing Responsibility

Once you have answered **yes** to giving your teenager more responsibility, it is time to follow through. There are many ways in which to provide them with practice.

### Chore Assignment

I am wary of putting this on the list, as it can easily be mishandled. However, chores help foster responsibility, accountability, and independence in teenagers. Assigning duties gives teenagers practice in tasks that will be solely their responsibility as an adult.

Assigning your teenager tasks encourages them to take accountability for things. If they do not do their chores, or if they do not do them properly, they will have to face the consequences. You determine these consequences. However, in the adult world, they will face the natural consequences of their actions or lack thereof. For example, not maintaining a home can lead to a highly unsafe and unhealthy environment.

It's imperative not to overwhelm and overload your teenager with chores or with responsibilities as a whole. After all, they still need to maintain their grades and interpersonal relationships. Give tasks in moderation to allow them to take the responsibility of fitting them into their lifestyle, not burdening them with unreasonable expectations.

**Establish Expectations**

First, let me clarify that expectations and conditions are not the same things. You can love your child unconditionally while having expectations for their life. Meeting (or surpassing) your *expectations* should not be a *condition* for your love.

Clearly outline for your teenager what is expected of them. Be just as clear in letting them know that, should they not meet expectations, there will be consequences, but you will not love them any less.

**Involve Them in Decision-Making**

Involving your teenager in making important decisions will introduce them to the idea that life is full of choices. It will give them a sense of responsibility and also a sense of importance in the family. Involve them in meal decisions, chore decisions, holiday destinations, essential purchases for the house, etc.

## Trust

Once you have given your teenager a responsibility, it is time to step back and trust that they will make the right decisions. This is difficult, especially if it is a responsibility that has been yours up until this point or one that, if done wrong, can cause them great strife. But it is now your teenager's responsibility. Give them the freedom and the trust to do with it the best they can.

## Consequences

As long as it is safe, do not protect your teenager from the consequences of their actions. Part of the responsibility is dealing with the results of inaction or wrong actions. If your teenager has made a decision that results in a consequence, they must face it head-on. This is how it will happen when they are adults, and they must get used to it now.

## Acknowledge the Successes

Life cannot always be about consequences and facing the negatives. If your teenager has made good decisions and acted the right way, they deserve to be appreciated for that. They are new to this; encouragement, when they succeed, will boost their confidence and urge them to continue making good decisions. There is no motivation if the only reward for making a good decision is simply not having to deal with bad consequences. Let your teenager know that you recognize when they have achieved something, that you are proud of them, and that you knew they were capable of it.

Here are some examples of encouraging language.

- "You're making progress."
- "I trust your judgment."
- "I need your help to do this."
- Any language that expresses that you know your teenager is capable.

Here are some examples of appreciative language.

- "You were a big help."
- "That was so thoughtful of you."
- "I really enjoyed that."

Here are some examples of how to let your teenager know they are working hard and improving.

- "I can see you've worked so hard on this."
- "Look at all the progress you have made."
- "I can see you are moving along."

It may seem unimportant to you, but it can make a world of difference in your teenager's life and confidence. We can all use a little motivation or appreciation.

**Help Them Plan for Success**

Sit down with your teenager and help them to plan out their future. They don't need a 2-year, 5-year, or 10-year mood board. They don't need to know what street they will live on and how many dogs they want. But they need to know what they are aiming for and their long-term goals. Knowing what you are working toward and trying to achieve in the *future* makes acting responsibly *now* much easier.

**Individuality**

You cannot begin to know every thought in your teenager's mind or every choice they will make. Your teenager is unique, and their decisions, goals, feelings, and values will be completely different from yours. Do not expect them to make the same decisions as you would and be supportive of the decisions they do make. They may be your flesh and blood; however, they have their own minds.

THINGS TEENS SHOULD BE DOING ON THEIR OWN

- Teenagers should be responsible for their sleep schedule. Teenagers should decide when to go to bed and when to wake up. You should not be waking your teenager up in the morning and telling them to get ready for school. You can set them up for success by helping them determine when to wake up and being there in the first week to help them adjust. There may be mornings when your teenager races out the door with less than a minute to spare, but they are ready for this responsibility. Let them deal with the natural consequences of sleeping in, such as missing the bus. They need to learn to be responsible for their decisions —the good ones and the bad ones.

- Your teenager should be making their breakfast and packing their lunch. At this point, they know what they do and don't like. While it may be *your* responsibility to ensure that there are healthy options in the house for your teenager, it should be their responsibility to put a decent breakfast and lunch together for themselves. You may be worried that your teenager is undereating, overeating, or choosing unhealthy options. However, they should make these mistakes while you are still around to guide them rather than when they are on their own in the adult world. You can set them up for success by giving them a list of items they should include, such as one sandwich, one healthy snack, one fun snack, and something to drink.

- In becoming independent and responsible, your teenager should take over the responsibility of washing their own clothes. You can buy their detergent and show them how to use the washing machine, but ensuring their clothes are clean, folded, packed away, and well-looked-after is up to them. If they do not take this responsibility seriously, they will soon face the natural consequence of not having clean clothes.

- Along with this comes the responsibility of cleaning their room. Your teenager's space and belongings are their responsibility. While their room is a safe place to express their true selves, it is important to teach them the responsibility of respecting their belongings. Sure, some people can live in a cluttered room, but it is not okay when that clutter starts turning into actual dirt and trash. Some people don't need to be very organized, but when their environment becomes unhealthy, that is not okay. You can set your teenager up by helping them to create a cleaning schedule that means they don't need to spend an entire Saturday making up for a month of not cleaning. One cleaning task a day will keep a room nice and tidy.

- The most important thing your teenager should be doing on their own is schoolwork, such as homework or assignments. Sure, they will need your help now and then or a motivating word to keep them going, but you should *never* be doing your child's schoolwork for them. There is absolutely *no* benefit to our children if we do their schoolwork for them. Their schoolwork is solely their responsibility, but we should be there to lend a helping hand when necessary. There are ways to intervene if there are academic shortcomings; however, none of these interventions include taking over the responsibility from them.

- Your teenager needs to be able to advocate for themselves. Teenagers should be able to stand up for themselves against bullies or peers. Your teenager should be responsible for calling on an authority figure's attention when necessary. If your teenager has a question about schoolwork, they should be able to talk to a teacher or coach without anxiety. When your teenager enters the workplace, they will be responsible for reporting to a superior; this is practice for that.

## CONSIDERATIONS

Is there a responsibility that you feel comfortable shifting onto your teenager? Why have you not given them that responsibility yet? If you are waiting for them to prove that they are ready, do they know they need to prove themselves?

Is there a responsibility you have given your teenager that they weren't ready for? Are you seeing them struggle with the consequences of not being up to that responsibility yet? How can you help them through that?

What are some responsibilities that your teenager wants to have but that you do not feel comfortable giving to them? Why? Is there a way for them to negotiate their way to a "yes"? If so, how?

# 7

# DISCIPLINING YOUR TEEN

Dylan's parents always allowed Dylan his independence and responsibility. They set boundaries for him, shifted responsibility to him, and allowed him to express his individuality and explore his personality. They prioritized keeping a solid relationship with him and did their best to communicate their way through problems.

However, to an unnecessary degree, Dylan's parents allowed him to deal with the consequences of his actions. Of course, this is important to do. We should not overprotect our teenagers or shield them from the consequences of their actions. But Dylan's parents did not protect him from consequences at all, nor did they enforce consequences when there were no natural ones.

If Dylan did not make himself lunch for the day, he didn't eat for the day, even if this happened every day for an entire week.

If Dylan was caught smoking, his parents believed the natural health consequences would urge him to stop. They didn't.

When Dylan was disrespectful to others, his parents did not intervene. When he was rude to *them*, they did not intervene. When Dylan would stay up all night watching television, his parents believed that the natural consequence of being tired would urge him to go to bed earlier. Instead, he would nap during school lessons or fall asleep for eight hours just as he got home from school, completely messing around his sleep cycle.

When Dylan stopped studying, started drinking alcohol, started skipping school, and broke every boundary they had set for him, his parents were at a loss as to how they had gone so wrong with him.

How could this situation have been different?

While it's true that natural consequences are the best way to teach your child responsibility, the natural consequences are sometimes not enough to send the message. Sometimes, consequences should be enforced by the parents. Occasionally, further discipline is necessary to stop a small problem from becoming more significant.

If Dylan's parents noticed that natural consequences were not working, they should have stepped in to discipline him. They should have removed some of his freedom and independence due to his irresponsibility and disrespect of the boundaries. They should have enforced related consequences to his misbehavior, such as taking away his television, giving him a bedtime, supervising his meals, or denying him social outings until his room was cleaned.

Sometimes teenagers need more than just natural consequences to get them to behave correctly. If you notice that your teen requires more discipline, you should provide it. A phrase often used is this: "If they want to act like a child, they should be treated like one." If they do not act with the responsibility and respect of a teenager, then they should not have the privilege of having the independence and freedom of a teenager.

## WHY DOES DISCIPLINE MATTER

### Discipline vs. Punishment

Discipline is the act of teaching your child how to think critically, make better decisions, and avoid further mistakes and misbehavior. Discipline does not equate to punishment. Discipline is necessary because it develops your teenager's critical thinking skills and encourages positive behavior.

Punishment often brings with it little to no improvement. Sure, a teenager may be punished for doing something wrong, but how often is that discipline effectively ensuring that behavior is left in the past? Discipline acts to teach your child *why* their actions were incorrect and *how* to avoid behaving similarly in the future.

## *Allow for Natural Consequences*

Here are a few things to keep in mind regarding the natural consequences of actions and behaviors:

- Natural consequences should only be allowed if they do not threaten a child's safety, health, or mental well-being. Living in a messy room is the natural consequence if your teenager does not keep their room neat. However, if your teenager is not cleaning their room to the point where there may be mold, pests, or other health risks, you should intervene and provide discipline.
- Natural consequences effectively teach teenagers that their actions are not solitary and will bring about repercussions. Being kind and respectful will offer you kindness and respect in return. It also means that avoiding homework and studying will bring about bad grades and the necessity for extra lessons.
- But natural consequences are sometimes not enough. They are sometimes too long-term or subtle for teenagers to learn from. Sometimes, they are prepared to deal with the natural consequence of their actions. Take budgeting, for example. The natural result of failing to budget your finances is that you won't have any money for the future. However, the future can be very far away, and having a decent lunch or a new phone is immediate gratification. Sometimes, your teenager may need more than the natural consequence to teach them that their behavior needs to change.

### Don't Make It About Something It Isn't

When your teenager has done something wrong—made a mistake, neglected a responsibility, broken a boundary—it's crucial to discipline for the most recent offense. When your teenager makes a mistake, it is not an invitation to drudge up every disagreement you have had with them. It is not an invitation to blame this unrelated thing on the one aspect of their personality you disagree with.

If your teenager skipped doing their washing last week and you decided to let it go, then you cannot bring it up when you are disciplining them about staying up late last night. If your teenager was penalized last month for not studying when they should have, you can't rehash that today when disciplining them for neglecting their chores.

Not only does this confuse your child about what exactly they did wrong, but it shows them that you keep a tally of all their wrong-doings—that their mistakes are what you choose to focus on. Bringing up other offenses while disciplining something else sends a message to your teenager that they would have been in trouble even if they had been responsible that day. Your teenager will begin to think that you are *always* upset with them.

If you intend to bring up past offenses every time they commit a new violation, you set yourself up for a very aggressive, long, and stagnant adolescent phase. This practice doesn't allow your teenager to blossom into their personality, learn from their mistakes, or develop self-confidence.

The goal is to teach them how to do better. This goal will be missed if you spend time bringing up irrelevant, already-dealt-with issues.

### Be a Guide

Once again, I return to the stallion metaphor. It may be tedious at this point, but I feel it is effective. Up until your child's teenage years, you have been with them on their little pony. It had its ups and downs and mood swings now and then, but whenever your child made a mistake or became overwhelmed and scared, you were right there to help them through it.

Except, "help" is a bit of a misnomer in this case. Because you often pulled the reins for them, controlling the pony for them. Hopefully, you walked them through how to do these things as you did so, but who's to say they paid attention?

Now, your teenager has upgraded to their very own stallion. You can no longer ride that horse with them. You can no longer pull the reins and calm the horse because it is your teen's responsibility. You are no longer a rule-maker, the only one in control.

You are now their guide, their teacher.

Your job as a parent, now, is to guide your teenager through their wild ride in life. Of course, your teenager may need you to steady their stallion with a whistle or block them from veering off the road. However, it is time for you to step back and watch as they ride off into their lives, making their own choices, pulling those reins in the wrong damn direction, but hey, it works for them.

Discipline does not involve climbing up onto your teenager's stallion. It does not include adjusting the stirrups and pulling the reins. All of that is now up to them. All they need is your support, your love, and your guidance.

## HOW TO DISCIPLINE TEENS

### *Crystal-Clear Expectations*

Your teenager will never meet your expectations if they do not know what those expectations are. Your teenager is less likely to strive to achieve your expectations if they don't fully understand them or why you decided they were necessary. They deserve to know what you expect of them and why.

How to talk about expectations:

- Clearly explain what you expect from your teenager.
- Clearly explain why this is what you expect and why it is crucial for them and you.
- Set them up for success by suggesting what they may need to do to meet these expectations; point out their responsibilities that correlate to these expectations.
- Be clear that you will be available to guide them, assist them, or offer advice when they need it.

- Be clear that, should they not meet your expectations, there will be consequences. Clearly explain what those consequences might be.
- Remind them that your love for them will never change or lessen if they do not meet your expectations. It's important to remind your teenager that you will love them unconditionally.

Something important to note in terms of setting expectations is not to overwhelm your teenager or bury them in stress. Make sure your expectations are reasonable, fair, and obtainable. Do not set impossibly high expectations. Only set expectations for that which is truly important and valuable for you. Too many expectations may overwhelm your teenager and confuse them about what they should prioritize.

Remember that your teenager is learning and developing. They will not knock it out of the park every single time. They are not going to do all their chores without complaint each day or get all As every semester. Do not expect impossibilities from them. Expect that they will do their best and be happy with that. By expecting too much, you set them up for failure, and you set yourself up for disappointment, which your teenager will believe they caused.

### Discipline Calmly

I know that the concept of discipline is embodied by a hunched-over, furrow-browed father shaking his fist in frustration. But that is not what discipline should be. Discipline shouldn't be aggressive or imposed with anger.

Your teenager is unlikely to listen to a word coming out of your mouth if you are coming at them aggressively. They are *learning.* When your child was learning to walk, you did not get angry when they stumbled. When your child was learning to talk, you did not get mad when they stuttered. That same love and shared interest in developing and improving should be offered to your teenager.

Sure, you had to catch them when they fell, you had to sound out the words, and you had to clean up midnight accidents. But you did it, kissed them goodnight, and went about your business. The same should be true with teenagers.

### *Grounding Is Not Dead*

When it is necessary, and when it is a related consequence, you should not be afraid to ground your teenager. Going out to parties is a privilege that can be taken away. Grounding is an old-school discipline technique that has been overused and abused. However, it remains effective.

Do not ground your teenager for unrelated or minor misbehavior. Ground your teenager for a reasonable amount of time, with reasonable restrictions, when it is appropriate. If you ground your teenager for a month and they misbehave again, will you ground them for another month?

### Deny Them Privileges

Privileges that can be denied when your teenager misbehaves:

- access to the internet (for non-school-related things)
- access to a cellphone
- access to a laptop, a television, or a gaming console
- freedom to leave the house and hang out with friends
- freedom to date or partake in romantic relationships
- having friends visit the house
- being allowed to drive and use the car
- freedom (to a degree)
- independence (to a degree)
- being allowed to take part in decision-making (to a degree)

Never take away your teenager's access to the home, bedroom, bathroom, or kitchen. They are entitled to clothing, access to bathroom facilities, a bed, shelter, food, etc. Do not remove a basic need as a means to discipline them. This goes beyond ineffective parenting and into the realm of abuse.

### Consequences Should Affect Them

We spoke about how some consequences are too subtle to change your teenager's behavior effectively. It would be best if you made sure that the consequences you impose as discipline affect your teenager. Discipline is not meant to be subtle or easy.

Discipline is supposed to be a negative consequence of your teenager's actions—emphasis on the *negative*. It should be upsetting, uncomfortable, and challenging. That is the whole point of facing your consequences.

If the discipline you try to employ is too subtle, easy, or comfortable, nothing stops your teenager from continuing their bad behavior because the consequences of their actions *weren't so bad*. Do not make it easy for your teenager.

The discipline you employ should dissuade your teenager from continuing bad behavior. They should not be willing to go through it again if it means they can continue their incorrect behavior. Your discipline must outweigh the negative behavior … significantly.

### My Roof, My Rules

It's an old saying I am sure we have all heard in our teenage years. "So long as you live under my roof, you will obey my rules." And to our chagrin, we realize that our parents were absolutely correct in saying that because it is true.

There are certain rules (not boundaries) that are simply non-negotiable. You may feel that your teenager is simply not allowed to partake in certain things—full stop (or *periodt*). These rules may be strict, or they may be less exact.

You may have a household rule that there will be no cussing tolerance. If your teenager does cuss, they have not obeyed a household rule and should receive discipline. You may have a household rule that leaves room for your teenager to make their own decisions. For example, you may have a rule that your teenager may drink alcohol but only two bottles of beer or nothing with an alcohol percentage higher than five. Rather than a hard-and-fast rule, it is simply a limit.

It is fair for you, as a parent, not to accept specific behaviors within your household. Just remember that these rules should be reasonable.

### *No Empty Threats*

If you have set clear expectations and boundaries and clearly explained the consequences of not abiding by those may be, you must follow through. As a parent, nothing will undercut your authority or your teenager's respect for you faster than an empty threat.

If you lay out a straightforward consequence of bad behavior but do not follow through, you are telling your teenager that you are "all bark and no bite." You send the message to your teenager that they can get away with anything because the consequences you laid out are just empty words.

Teenagers will lose respect for their parents quickly if they do not follow through on disciplining them to the full effect. Often, this disrespect grows and grows the longer you do not put your money where your mouth is. Teenagers will very quickly start to take advantage and take authority in the house because, to them, you have proved that you do not have the power.

### Consistency Is Key

For the same reason, being consistent in your discipline is important. If you do not accept a particular behavior, you cannot let it slide when you feel like it. If you let this behavior slide, you cannot suddenly discipline them for it. Doing so will belittle your authority, as well as confuse your teenager.

## WHAT IF THEY IGNORE THE CONSEQUENCES?

Even with the best intentions, and the best chance at success, parenting a teen can be difficult. Finding a way to discipline them effectively can seem nearly impossible. Sometimes, no matter what the consequence of their actions is, it doesn't seem to stick with them or encourage them to change their behavior.

Perhaps your teenager is acting out. You have tried to let them face the natural consequences, but that had little effect. You decided to discipline them using your consequences, but that didn't do it either. Your teenager seems hell-bent on continuing to behave negatively.

There are some things to consider when setting out consequences for your teenager. The first of those things is how much meaning and weight the consequence carries. If your teenager does not actively use the television in their room, removing it will not affect their behavior. If your teenager does not care about going out to parties, then grounding them will not affect their behavior.

It would be best if you chose a consequence appropriate for the situation and level of misbehavior, which will actually affect your teenager's life. If you are worried that you may not be able to find something that matches, make a list of possibilities in advance. If the time comes that you need to discipline them, you choose a consequence off of your list.

When disciplining your child, do not attempt to tug on their heartstrings. Do not try to appeal to their emotions or make them feel guilty. Do not try to convince them that they would change their behavior if they "cared" more or "loved" more.

First, this is ineffective. Second, this is emotional manipulation. Your job as a parent is to discipline, not try to change their minds or feelings. Simply follow through with the discipline.

Do not let your discipline or consequence be a gray area of debate or discussion. Keep your consequences clear, simple, and straightforward. If your teenager does this, then this happens as a result. Do not add too many clauses, conditions, or exceptions to your disciplines. Do not make the triggering event of discipline confusing, unclear, or debatable. If your teenager does *this thing*, then the consequence is *that thing* —simple.

This practice helps to keep your discipline consistent. Because every time your teenager does the thing, they get the relevant discipline. It closes any gaps where your teenager may try to debate, negotiate, or argue their way out of a consequence. It gives you the confidence to avoid being pulled into an unnecessary argument.

If the consequence of their actions is grounding, avoid the perfunctory timeline nonsense. Do not ground your child by pulling a random date out of your pocket and saying they are grounded until then. How do you measure disrespect in days? How do you measure boundary-breaking in days? At what point is the grounding term unreasonable?

Instead, give your teenager a goal or a task. They are grounded until they do or learn a particular thing. Make your consequences task-orientated rather than time-orientated. Grounding does not have to be a week-long endeavor. And what exactly do you expect your teenager to do without their phone or computer?

Set your teenager a task and a goal, and once they have achieved or completed it, they are effectively ungrounded.

Last, change the consequence if you notice it is not affecting their behavior. We spoke about consistency, but if it isn't working, consistency won't matter anyway. Explain to your teenager that the other consequence was not teaching them to change their behavior, and you will continue to try new discipline techniques until they do learn.

## CONSIDERATIONS

Have you been inconsistent with discipline recently? Have you let something slide that you would usually try to correct? Have you disciplined for something that you usually would have allowed? Why?

Is your teenager unresponsive to your current disciplinary methods? How can you adjust your strategies so the consequences have more weight and effectiveness?

# 8

# DON'T FORGET TO TAKE CARE OF YOURSELF

**April's Mother's POV:**

April's mother is growing increasingly stressed. April has been impossible to deal with lately. It feels like every time she opens her mouth to talk, she has somehow offended her daughter. April no longer eats out in the dining room. She no longer does her homework in the office. It feels like April is slowly drifting away.

Unfortunately, this brings unresolved trauma from April's mother's life. April's mother has abandonment anxiety. Her daughter pulling away and finding her own life is causing her a lot of stress. However, April's mother knows that this behavior is normal and healthy. Of course, she wants her teenager to become independent and responsible. She is so proud to see her daughter growing into a beautiful woman. The feeling of abandonment is accompanied by guilt and disappointment in herself. She should not be feeling abandoned by her teenager growing up. She knows that April is not leaving her.

On top of this, April's mother is very overworked. She is on the brink of burnout but uses work as a coping mechanism for her depression. She is working herself to the bone and burying herself under so much stress that she is starting to lose weight.

**April's POV:**

April is acutely aware of her mother's decline. Her mom is losing weight, going pale, and hasn't eaten a proper meal in weeks. It breaks her heart to see her mother being so sad. She is filled with guilt and depression, thinking that she is probably the cause of her mother's strife.

April doesn't eat with her mother anymore because it breaks her heart to see how little food her mom dishes up for herself. April doesn't talk to her mother anymore because half of their conversations end with her mother in tears.

April is already dealing with a lot in her own life, and she does not feel prepared, capable, or knowledgeable enough to deal with her mother's decline. It's best for her to avoid and detach from her mother, giving her space to heal.

How could this situation have been different?

April's mother is neglecting her self-care and her own mental well-being. April is watching her mother slowly decline, and it is causing her depression as well. April and her mom's relationship is starting to sever. April is not seeing a healthy example of how to look after herself and maintain her own mental health effectively.

If April's mother had focused more on healing herself, taking care of herself, and maintaining her mental health, she would be better positioned to be there for her daughter. Of course, maintaining mental well-being is sometimes easier said than done. However, it becomes increasingly difficult to take care of your children when you neglect yourself.

## TO BE A GOOD PARENT, YOU MUST TAKE CARE OF YOURSELF

Have you ever caught yourself saying something to your teenager that your parents used to say to you? Has one of those things ever stuck with you for years in a hostile, self-conscious, traumatic way? Do you recognize signs that you are continuing and perpetuating generational trauma?

We cannot be effective and loving parents if we have not spent the time to heal and recover from trauma in our life. The teenage years are difficult for almost everyone, and for many of us, that turns into lifelong mental unhealthiness that must be addressed and resolved.

If you want to bring up the best version of your teenager, you need to be the best version of yourself. If you are triggered by conflict, you may find yourself avoiding the discipline of your teenagers. If you have unresolved anger, you may find yourself acting with too much aggression toward your teenagers. If you struggle with a specific aspect of life due to your poor mental health, you cannot effectively guide your teenager in that aspect of life. Worse, you may inadvertently teach them unhealthy habits and behaviors.

Being a parent is an opportunity to heal ourselves, to do better than our parents did with us, and to steer our children away from experiencing that same trauma.

The first step in achieving this is to parent mindfully and consciously. Make a conscious effort to recognize when we are reacting unfairly toward our teenagers. Sometimes we overreact, are not attentive, or are triggered by something and need to do some reflecting. Often, it is our own stress and frustration that causes us to react to our children. Of course, sometimes the actions of our children warrant and deserve a reaction, but sometimes we may discipline where it isn't necessary because of our stressful day.

Amazingly, the reverse also happens. Sometimes, a parent becomes unresponsive and irresponsible as they avoid disciplining their children. Maybe when they were a child, they were punished at every turn for every small thing and vowed they would not do the same with their children. However, they go too far in the opposite direction and allow their children to get away with almost everything.

If you recognize yourself reacting inappropriately (whether that means not reacting at all or reacting with too much aggression), press pause. Take a moment to collect your thoughts and tell yourself what might happen if you react the way you want to. Assess if it will be healthy and if it will teach your child effectively. If you need a moment, take a moment; walk out of the room and regroup.

Show your child an example of healthy self-regulation and anger management. This is how you show your teenager to act with the consequences of your actions in mind and break the cycle of ineffective parenting.

The truth is that intense emotions can sometimes cause us to say and do things we wouldn't normally do. We may react ineffectively or incorrectly when triggered by anger or depression. When your body goes into "fight or flight" mode, it is easy to think of your child as the enemy, as the cause of this distress. You may feel that they deserve to be disciplined because it is not okay for them to have made you this upset.

But, once again, this is our own trauma clouding our judgment. Be aware of your emotions, what triggers them, what they make you want to do, and how to calm them so that you can be a parent first.

As parents, we must look back on our childhood with the wise eyes of an adult and as a parent. We must reflect and analyze our childhood and correct our teenage thoughts and conclusions. We need to recognize what was trauma and not our fault or within our control. If we have misconceptions about why our parents treated us a certain way, we can look back on those instances and recognize that our parents were reacting to their own emotions and not our behavior. We can realize that the self-doubt or self-hatred we felt was misplaced because that behavior had nothing to do with us.

By doing this, we can identify where we are doing the same thing—reacting to our emotions rather than to our child's behavior. We can prevent ourselves from scarring our children as our parents scarred us.

Once we have recognized our triggers, traumas, behaviors, and problems to work through, it is time to heal. It is time to do some self-care and prioritize de-stressing and looking after ourselves. This is perhaps the most critical part of this section. Learning to look after yourself, see to your own needs, and regulate your emotions will inadvertently teach your teenager to do the same.

Much of mental unwellness comes from the lack of self-care and compassion. Self-doubt, self-consciousness, and self-hatred can become so all-consuming that we either don't think we deserve to be cared for or don't know how to start caring for ourselves. We need to practice self-care and emotional decompression to teach our teenagers to do the same in times of mental unwellness.

If you recognize that your problem has gone too far and that you have tried to de-stress and do self-care but nothing is helping you to heal, there is no shame in seeking professional help. If not for your own sake, then for your teenager's.

## SELF-CARE FOR PARENTS

### *Physical Self-Care*

- Be active and exercise regularly. A healthy body facilitates a healthy mind. You can exercise on your own, but you can also find a way to include your whole family, including your teenagers. Exercise does not have to be a mindless hour in the gym; it could be your entire family having swimming races in the pool. Teach your children to stay active.
- Sleep is one of those things that affect us daily and immensely. People forget that not getting enough sleep can affect your mood, mental health, and physical well-being. Practice a healthy sleep schedule because something as small as just getting enough will significantly increase your mood and overall health.
- As a parent, you are responsible for ensuring that your children have a healthy and balanced diet. This means that you should be eating healthy foods regularly as well.
- Look after your body with skincare, hair care, and even massages to destress. You do not need to book a day at the spa, but you would be surprised how much tension can be relieved from a good back massage.
- The human body is a big fan of physical contact; getting a hug can make everything feel better. Spend some time cuddling with your children. Or spend some time being affectionate with your partner, cuddling, kissing, and

making love to them. When those physical affection needs are met, you will automatically feel better.

- Destress with a long steaming shower or bath. There is little that feels better than spending time soaking in a hot bath and feeling fresh and clean coming out.
- Treat yourself to a calming hot cup of tea or hot chocolate.

### Emotional and Social Self-Care

- Make an active effort to prioritize your friendships. Go out with your friends, or invite them over for tea. It can become very isolating to be surrounded by your children or work colleagues with no challenging or intelligent conversation.
- Prioritize your alone time. Take a moment each day to recenter and reground yourself in isolation. Spend some time away from the hustle and bustle of your children and spend some time on your own thoughts, feelings, and reflections. Use positive self-talk such as "take it easy," "this will pass," or "everything will be okay."
- Include doing things that make you happy in your every day. If you like gardening, ensure you are in your garden for five minutes daily. If you like reading, make sure to read every day. Prioritize doing the things that make you happy.
- Do not bottle up or internalize big emotions. Allow yourself to go through the motions, feel your feelings, and cry.

- Find things in each day that make you smile and laugh —things that make you appreciative.
- Do not forget to prioritize your relationship. It is easy for parents to neglect their partner because children consume our whole world. Make time in your week for romantic dates with your partner, cuddling and kissing, and making love. Remember that your partner is there when you need someone to hold you.
- Do not overwork or overwhelm yourself. Do not take on extra responsibilities if you do not have the capacity for them. There is no shame in saying no. Do not accept responsibilities that would bring you more stress than peace.

### Intellectual Self-Care

- While driving around, cleaning the house, or doing monotonous chores, listen to an audiobook, a podcast, or a radio station covering a topic of interest.
- Find a way to express your thoughts and feelings— journaling, writing stories, creating a blog post, etc. Find a way to ensure your thoughts are not trapped inside your head.
- Watch documentaries on new and exciting topics.
- Make yourself complete a project that is exciting, rewarding, and challenging.
- Make time for hobbies you have not done since your child was born—old hobbies that you never fell out of love with may still bring the same joy and happiness as they used to.

## TEACHING YOUR TEEN SELF-CARE

The first step to teaching your teenager self-care is teaching them precisely what self-care is. You may think that self-care is self-explanatory; however, your teenager may not know they are allowed to look after themselves. Self-care is about identifying physical and emotional needs and working toward getting those needs met.

The emphasis of self-care is on the *self* aspect of it. Self-care is taking responsibility for meeting your own needs, looking after yourself, and being able to do it yourself. Of course, as parents, we should ensure that they know we will always be there if they need help and guidance. But self-care is a personal journey.

Like you, your teenager needs to know how to take care of their physical needs.

- maintaining personal hygiene
- staying active and moving
- looking after their bodies
- dressing themselves
- maintaining their hair
- recognizing when they are dehydrated or hungry
- getting enough sleep

Children need to know that a healthy and looked-after body will facilitate a healthy mind.

It's also essential for teenagers to learn and recognize that they can enjoy their time and have fun without being behind a screen. Not all entertainment is on a screen. There are plenty of ways to be productive and have a great time without a phone in their hands.

They will loathe hearing this, but it is not healthy for teenagers to spend so much time on their phones. Simply getting away from the buzz of social media and the internet can be extremely valuable to their mental health; it can be an act of self-care. Things to do away from their phone may include:

- art
- writing or poetry
- sculpting
- sports
- exercise and outdoor activities
- house maintenance and home improvement
- gardening

The best way to help your teenager and guide them through effective self-care is to develop a healthy routine for you, them, and the family. Make sure the self-care is a scheduled part of their every day; this will hold them accountable and keep them responsible for ensuring they do not neglect their self-care. This also helps your teenager turn self-care into a habit that they do every day without issue.

Try the following:

- Have a scheduled no-phone time where everyone in the family preoccupies themselves with a task that does not require their phone.

- Have meal times at consistent and regular times.
- Suggest a window in which your teenager prioritizes personal hygiene and cleaning their space.
- Schedule a daily outdoor activity with your children to get them active and out into the fresh air.

Encourage your teenager to take mental health breaks when they are needed. Keep an eye out for burnout and overwhelm because it is difficult to recognize it in the moment. Encourage your teenager to have an hour of downtime each day and get a lot of rest when necessary.

## CONSIDERATIONS

Can you recognize an area in your life where you have not fully healed; where it may be affecting how you parent your children?

Can you identify situations where your trauma and stress affected your discipline or parenting technique? Can you identify any cases where your trauma and stress negatively impacted your child?

Are you willing and prepared to work on yourself, look after and care for yourself, and be the best parent you can be for your children?

How do you plan on incorporating self-care into your and your child's routine? How do you plan on prioritizing your own healing?

# CONCLUSION

It is time to help your baby get up onto their own stallion and send them off down that road of life. You have done what you can; you have taught them as much as you can about how to control their wild stallion. You have set up the fences, guarded them against those dangerous areas, and given them your unconditional love.

It's important to remember that none of the parenting tips in this book will make this process smooth like butter. All roads of life have pesky sharp stones, inconvenient boulders, and huge potholes to maneuver around, and no two roads of life are the same. However, the tips in the book should make the process easier.

In conclusion, remember to:

- Make an effort to understand your teenager—what they are feeling, what they are going through, and perhaps why they make the choices they sometimes make.
- Never neglect communication. Communication can help someone through even the toughest of times. It can help you avoid mistakes and arguments and better understand your teenager. The more you communicate with them, the more you will appreciate them.
- Set and enforce boundaries with relevant and natural consequences. Choose limits that work for you, your teenager, and your family. Use these boundaries to ensure your teenager acts according to your family values.
- Make an effort to maintain and build a strong connection with your teenager. Now is not the time to pull away. Instead, be there for your teenager more than ever—even if it is not in the way you were expecting.
- Offer your teenager more responsibilities, allowing them the freedom to find their independence, prove their capabilities, and practice for adulthood.
- Never neglect to provide discipline when it is needed. Have a firm, fair hand in making sure your teenager has no misconceptions about what is right and what is wrong.
- Take care of yourself during this time. It can be heartbreaking to see your child starting to grow up and become independent. Recognize that sense of loss that

you are feeling, and do not neglect yourself in this process.

Most importantly, remember that your teenager is only learning. They will make mistakes, and you will fall short too. Together, you can both grow and improve.

# A GIFT TO OUR READERS

Included with your purchase of this book is our short Parents'
Guide
## How To Help Your Teen Fight Anxiety, Stress and Depression

## Scan QR code or visit:

### keepyourcool.littlegeckopublishing.com

# REFERENCES

AACAP. (2016, September). *Teen brain: Behavior, problem solving, and decision making*. AACAP. https://www.aacap.org/aacap/families_and_youth/facts_for_families/fff-guide/the-teen-brain-behavior-problem-solving-and-decision-making-095.aspx

American Psychological Association. (2017, June). *Parenting styles*. APA. https://www.apa.org/act/resources/fact-sheets/parenting-styles

Amunategui, L. F. (2019, May 8). *You can have a strong relationship with your teen here's how*. University Hospitals. https://www.uhhospitals.org/Healthy-at-UH/articles/2019/05/you-can-have-a-strong-relationship-with-your-teen-heres-how

Barendse, M. E. A., Cheng, T. W., & Pfeifer, J. H. (2020). *Your Brain on Puberty*. Frontiers for Young Minds, 8(53). https://doi.org/10.3389/frym.2020.00053

Betz, M. (2021, April 21). *What is self-awareness, and why is it important?* BetterUp. https://www.betterup.com/blog/what-is-self-awareness

Brennan, D. (2021, March 9). *What is authoritarian parenting?* WebMD. https://www.webmd.com/parenting/authoritarian-parenting-what-is-it

Cherry, K. (2019, July 17). *Uninvolved parenting and its effects on children*. Verywell Mind. https://www.verywellmind.com/what-is-uninvolved-parenting-2794958

Churchill, J. (1992). *Grime and punishment*. Avon Books.

*Communicating with teenagers*. (n.d.). Skills You Need. https://www.skillsyouneed.com/parent/communicating-with-teenagers.html

Davies, P. (2021, February 3). *How controlling your tone of voice affects your children*. Moms. https://www.moms.com/how-controlling-voice-tone-affects-children/

Devine, M. (2019). *How to talk to teens: 3 ways to get your teen to listen*. Empowering Parents. https://www.empoweringparents.com/article/how-to-talk-to-teens-3-ways-to-get-your-teen-to-listen/

Dewar, G. (2017a, June 2). *Authoritarian parenting: What happens to the kids?* Parenting Science. https://parentingscience.com/authoritarian-parenting/

Dewar, G. (2017b, July 2). *The authoritative parenting style: An evidence-based guide.* Parenting Science. https://parentingscience.com/authoritative-parenting-style/

Ditch the Label. (2020, March 23). *10 tips for parents - how to speak to your teenage son.* Ditch the Label. https://www.ditchthelabel.org/10-tips-parents-speak-teenage-son/

Enan, R. (2022, January 10). *The newest teen slang trends of 2021.* Family Education. https://www.familyeducation.com/teens/newest-teen-slang-trends-2021

Gongala, S. (2021, February 23). *How to discipline teenagers? 8 tips that will work.* MomJunction. https://www.momjunction.com/articles/format-how-to-discipline-teenagers_00713799/

Gordon, S. (2021, July 26). *Everything your teen needs to know about setting boundaries.* Verywell Family. https://www.verywellfamily.com/boundaries-what-every-teen-needs-to-know-5119428

Gould, S. (2019, January 14). *8 ways to connect with your teenage son when he won't talk to you.* Moms of Tweens and Teens. https://momsoftweensandteens.com/how-can-i-get-my-teenage-boy-to-talk/

Gregston, M. (n.d.). *Why your teen needs boundaries.* Focus on the Family. https://www.focusonthefamily.ca/content/why-your-teen-needs-boundaries

Hamilton, J. (2014, August 26). *The importance of building a relationship with your teen.* Doorways. https://doorwaysarizona.com/importance-building-relationship-teen/

Heston, K. (2021, May 6). *3 ways to discipline a teenager.* WikiHow. https://www.wikihow.com/Discipline-a-Teenager

Hopkins, C. (2016, January 23). *Teenager parent relationship: How to build a healthy relationship.* Psych Central. https://psychcentral.com/blog/5-tips-for-building-a-healthy-relationship-with-your-teenager#2

*How to teach your children about self care.* (2019, May 20). Community Access Network. https://www.communityaccessnetwork.org/how-to-teach-your-children-about-self-care/

Janelled. (2019). *Self-Care for parents.* Peps. https://www.peps.org/ParentResources/by-topic/self-care/self-care-for-parents

Jantz, G. L. (2014, April 11). *9 tips for communicating with your teenage son.* Psychology Today. https://www.psychologytoday.com/us/blog/hope-relationships/201404/9-tips-communicating-your-teenage-son

Jolly, J. (2018, August 10). *"It's lit": The ultimate guide to decoding your teen's text and speak.* USA TODAY. https://www.usatoday.com/story/tech/colum nist/2018/08/10/ultimate-guide-understanding-teen-slang-and-text/ 936280002/

Krause, N. (n.d.). *Emotional changes during puberty.* Always. https://www.always.co.uk/en-gb/tips-and-advice-for-girls-and-parents/my-body/emotional-changes-during-puberty/

Kwan, E. (2018, October 25). *How to connect with a teen that doesn't want to talk.* Hand in Hand Parenting. https://www.handinhandparenting.org/2018/10/how-to-talk-to-teenager/

LaScala, M. (2019, March 14). *Everything you need to know about the free-range parenting method.* Good Housekeeping. https://www.goodhousekeeping.com/life/parenting/a26824973/free-range-parenting/

Lee, K. (2021, July 13). *Keep tone and words positive when communicating with your child.* Verywell Family. https://www.verywellfamily.com/how-do-you-talk-to-your-child-620058#citation-1

Lehman, J. (2011). *Kids who ignore consequences: 10 ways to make them stick.* Empowering Parents. https://www.empoweringparents.com/article/kids-who-ignore-consequences-10-ways-to-make-them-stick/

Li, P. (2020, October 8). *Uninvolved parenting - why it's the worst parenting style.* Parenting for Brain. https://www.parentingforbrain.com/uninvolved-parenting/

Li, P. (2021, October 13). *How to discipline a teenager who doesn't care about consequences.* Parenting for Brain. https://www.parentingforbrain.com/how-to-discipline-a-teenager-who-doesnt-care-about-consequences/

Markham, L. (n.d.). *Being parents gives us an opportunity to heal ourselves.* Aha! Parenting. https://www.ahaparenting.com/read/healing-yourself

Martin, J. (2020, May 14). *5 reasons why teenagers don't listen.* All pro Dad. https://www.allprodad.com/5-reasons-why-teenagers-dont-listen/

Mayer, D. J. (2014, April 29). *The discipline tool box: 15 tips for effective discipline.* Your Teen Magazine. https://yourteenmag.com/family-life/discipline/disciplining-your-teen

Menstrupedia. (2019). *Emotional changes that occur during puberty.* Menstrupedia. https://www.menstrupedia.com/articles/girls/emotional-changes

Morin, A. (n.d.). *7 ways to help teens and tweens gain self-awareness.* Understood.

https://www.understood.org/en/articles/7-ways-to-help-teens-and-tweens-gain-self-awareness

Morin, A. (2019). *Teen slang words every parent should know.* Verywell Family. https://www.verywellfamily.com/a-teen-slang-dictionary-2610994

Morin, A. (2020, November 21). *How free-range parenting can benefit your child.* Verywell Family. https://www.verywellfamily.com/what-is-free-range-parenting-1095057

Myers, M. (2017, August 13). *10 ways to build A ROCK SOLID relationship with your tween or teen.* Sunshine and Hurricanes. https://www.sunshineandhurricanes.com/building-a-relationship-with-your-teen/

Pickhardt, C. E. (2019, July 19). *How parents can teach adolescents responsibility.* Psychology Today. https://www.psychologytoday.com/us/blog/surviving-your-childs-adolescence/202107/how-parents-can-teach-adolescents-responsibility

Pontz, E. (2018, September 4). *7 smart tips for setting boundaries.* Center for Parent and Teen Communication. https://parentandteen.com/7-smart-tips-for-setting-boundaries-for-your-teenager/

Pradeep. (2017, January 7). *12 behavioral similarities between a toddler and a teenager.* Being the Parent. https://www.beingtheparent.com/toddler-teenager-similarities/

Price-Mitchell, M. (2016, April 6). *Teach your teen to set emotional boundaries.* Psychology Today. https://www.psychologytoday.com/us/blog/the-moment-youth/201904/teach-your-teen-set-emotional-boundaries

Raising Children Network. (2019, October 17). *Independence in teenagers: How to support it.* Raising Children Network. https://raisingchildren.net.au/pre-teens/development/social-emotional-development/independence-in-teens

*Responsibilities teens should be doing independently.* (2020, February 17). Middle Earth. https://middleearthnj.org/2020/02/17/responsibilities-teens-should-be-doing-independently/

Reynolds, N. (2020, February 5). *The verdict: Parenting teenagers isn't easier than parenting toddlers, it just morphs into a different version of worrying.* Raising Teens Today. https://raisingteenstoday.com/the-verdict-parenting-teenagers-isnt-easier-than-parenting-toddlers-it-just-morphs-into-a-different-version-of-worrying/

Rodgers, K. B. (n.d.). *What to know about teen independence.* The University of Tennessee Agricultural Extension Service. https://extension.tennessee.

edu/publications/Documents/sp491a.pdf

Schoolhouse. (2019, October 17). *Reasons why it is so important to encourage independence in children.* Schoolhouse Day Care. https://schoolhouse-daycare.co.uk/blog/why-you-should-encourage-independence/

*Set realistic boundaries with your teenager.* (n.d.). Reachout.com. https://parents.au.reachout.com/skills-to-build/connecting-and-communicating/things-to-try-building-trust/set-realistic-boundaries-with-your-teenager

Shameer, M. (2015, February 10). *11 tips to make your teen independent and yet keep close to you.* MomJunction. https://www.momjunction.com/articles/tips-to-make-your-teenager-independent_00327305/

*Shifting responsibility to your child: Teenage years.* (2018, May 3). Raising Children Network. https://raisingchildren.net.au/pre-teens/communicating-relationships/family-relationships/shifting-responsibility-teen-years

Shohamy, D., Foerde, K., Davidow, J., & Galván, A. (2016, October 5). *Brain study reveals how teens learn differently than adults.* Columbia | Zuckerman Institute. https://zuckermaninstitute.columbia.edu/brain-study-reveals-how-teens-learn-differently-adults

Shout Out UK. (2021, July 8). *The importance of being independent.* Shout out UK. https://www.shoutoutuk.org/2021/07/08/the-importance-of-being-independent/

Staff, D. (2021, July 2). *The importance of being independent.* Delaware Psychological Services. https://www.delawarepsychologicalservices.com/post/the-importance-of-being-independent

Suttie, J. (2016). *What adolescents really need from parents.* Greater Good. https://greatergood.berkeley.edu/article/item/what_adolescents_really_need_from_parents

The Bark Team. (2021, March 2). *2021 teen slang meanings every parent should know.* Bark. https://www.bark.us/blog/teen-text-speak-codes-every-parent-should-know/

Trautner, T. (2017). *Permissive parenting style.* MSU Extension. https://www.canr.msu.edu/news/permissive_parenting_style

Wang, M.-T., & Kenny, S. (2013). Longitudinal links between fathers' and mothers' harsh verbal discipline and adolescents' conduct problems and depressive symptoms. *Child Development, 85*(3), 908–923. https://doi.org/10.1111/cdev.12143

*Why some teens hate their parents.* (n.d.). Online Parenting Coach. https://www.onlineparentingcoach.com/2012/10/why-some-teens-hate-their-parents.html

Whyte, A. (2019, March 4). *The importance of giving kids responsibilities.* Evolve Treatment Centers. https://evolvetreatment.com/blog/giving-kids-responsibilities/

Zeltser, F. (2021, October 5). *Here's what makes "authoritative parents" different from the rest—and why psychologists say it's the best parenting style.* CNBC. https://www.cnbc.com/2021/10/05/child-psychologist-explains-why-authoritative-parenting-is-the-best-style-for-raising-smart-confident-kids.html

**Atribution**

Book cover has been designed using assets from Freepik.com

<a href="https://www.freepik.com/free-vector/chaos-room-with-calm-mother-adorable-naughty-children-female-person-with-mischievous-kids-flat-vector-illustration-family-motherhood-concept-banner-website-design-landing-web-page_26876748.htm#query=kids%20mess-ing%20house&position=30&from_view=search&track=sph">Image by pch.vector</a> on Freepik

<a href="https://www.freepik.com/free-vector/dirty-room-interior-compo-sition-with-indoor-view-living-room-with-decorations-wall-paintings-rubbish-vector-illustration_31756199.htm#query=mess%20house&posi-tion=5&from_view=search&track=sph">Image by macrovector</a> on Freepik

<a href="https://www.freepik.com/free-vector/organic-flat-people-meditat-ing_13295507.htm#page=4&query=meditation&posi-tion=35&from_view=search&track=sph">Image by pikisuperstar</a> on Freepik

<a href="https://www.freepik.com/free-vector/funny-people-listening-music-using-headphones-isolated-colored-icons-set-flat-vector-illustra-tion_26766011.htm#query=teen%20listen%20to%20music&posi-tion=8&from_view=search&track=sph">Image by macrovector</a> on Freepik

Image by <a href="https://www.freepik.com/free-vector/hand-drawn-black-speaker-background_4471596.htm#query=loud%20speaker&posi-tion=3&from_view=search&track=sph">Freepik</a>

Made in United States
Troutdale, OR
11/18/2024

24975517R00086